JESUS WAS DIFFERENT

JESUS WAS DIFFERENT

SPIRITUAL GROWTH THROUGH ACTUALLY FOLLOWING THE TEACHINGS OF JESUS

BROOKS DRIVER

WESTBOW
PRESS®
A DIVISION OF THOMAS NELSON
& ZONDERVAN

Copyright © 2024 Brooks Driver.

All rights reserved. No part of this book may be used or reproduced by any means, graphic, electronic, or mechanical, including photocopying, recording, taping or by any information storage retrieval system without the written permission of the author except in the case of brief quotations embodied in critical articles and reviews.

This book is a work of non-fiction. Unless otherwise noted, the author and the publisher make no explicit guarantees as to the accuracy of the information contained in this book and in some cases, names of people and places have been altered to protect their privacy.

WestBow Press books may be ordered through booksellers or by contacting:

WestBow Press
A Division of Thomas Nelson & Zondervan
1663 Liberty Drive
Bloomington, IN 47403
www.westbowpress.com
844-714-3454

Because of the dynamic nature of the Internet, any web addresses or links contained in this book may have changed since publication and may no longer be valid. The views expressed in this work are solely those of the author and do not necessarily reflect the views of the publisher, and the publisher hereby disclaims any responsibility for them.

Any people depicted in stock imagery provided by Getty Images are models, and such images are being used for illustrative purposes only. Certain stock imagery © Getty Images.

All Scripture quotations are from the ESV® Bible (The Holy Bible, English Standard Version®), copyright © 2001 by Crossway, a publishing ministry of Good News Publishers. Used by permission. All rights reserved.

ISBN: 979-8-3850-3467-3 (sc)
ISBN: 979-8-3850-3469-7 (hc)
ISBN: 979-8-3850-3468-0 (e)

Library of Congress Control Number: 2024920753

Print information available on the last page.

WestBow Press rev. date: 10/03/2024

DEDICATION

This book is dedicated to my incredible wife, Lauren. Thank you for loving Jesus, myself, and our children. Without you, this book would still be a far-off dream of mine.

CONTENTS

Introduction ix

1	Jesus Was Different	1
2	The Worst Quote Ever	9
3	Is It Cake?	21
4	Only the Servants Knew	31
5	Martha, Martha	40
6	Burn and Scuttle the Boats	52
7	In Play at Little Games	63
8	The Prince of Peace Wielding a Sword	76
9	Consistent and Persistent	86
10	Hell Is Real	97
11	Turn the World Upside Down	107

Endnotes 125

INTRODUCTION

If you are reading this, I want you to know I am honored that you would pick up this book. As I type this right now I am praying for you. No, I may not know you; but God does, and he cares for you more than you could ever imagine. I believe that my prayers for you will be answered and that this book will help you know God and grow in your relationship with him. Would you take a quick moment to pray for yourself? Ask the Lord God to help you see how he sees and live the life he wills for you. Pray that you will learn exactly what God wants you to learn from this book and that you would apply it to your life.

Actually, that's how this book came to fruition. I prayed for similar things myself when I realized I needed to make some changes in my life with Christ. I started to look at the way that Jesus lived and to be honest, my life wasn't lining up. I took it a step further and observed the people around me who were also believers in Jesus, and again, some things just looked different compared to the way Jesus lived. I struggled with this, and still do. I went on a journey of seeking Jesus and how to live like him, and I found that Jesus was very different. What I found was a big enough deal that led me to writing this book, and I hope for you it is a big enough deal to read it.

I want to be upfront with you. Some of these chapters might be challenging to you and may be hard to hear. Sometimes the truth is a tough pill to swallow, but the truth will also set you free. Proverbs 27:5-6 says, *"Better is open rebuke than hidden love. Faithful are the wounds of a friend; profuse are the kisses of an enemy."*[1] If I wound you with my words, know that it comes from a friend in Christ with much love. Also, know that these are truths from the Bible that are without fault or blemish.

As you read, I challenge you to put aside all your fears, doubts, church-hurt, what your dad told you, your unbelief, pride, sins, and anything else that you think might hinder you from receiving the truth of what life with Jesus looks like. By doing this, you will open your hands, mind, and most importantly your spirit to receive what I believe God has for you in this book. I am excited and expectant for you on this journey of stepping into a more intentional life that looks more like Jesus than ever before.

CHAPTER 1

Jesus Was Different

Have you ever thought about how the life of Jesus was so polarizing? How could this man named Jesus make such a big difference in the world? Over 2000 years later, people are still talking about him and even following him. In 1971, *Time Magazine* even put an image of Jesus on their cover because of a revolution and revival happening across America...about Jesus.[2] Why is he so loved by some and so hated by others? If he was only a man, why and how did he have such a big impact on the world? Well, we know that he was not only a man but he was God incarnate. He proved his deity in many ways, one of which by the way that he lived. It would have been impossible for anyone but God himself to live in the manor that Jesus lived. He was so unique to the rest of the world, not only in his person, but simply how he went about life. Even today when we look at the way that Jesus lived compared to others, it was quite different.

Don't get me wrong, he lived a normal life in ways. He worked as a carpenter, was a Jewish man like his surrounding community, and he had friends and family around him. He lived in a small town called Nazareth and people knew him and his parents. Have you ever wondered what Jesus' childhood was like? He probably played with his siblings, said the Hebrew prayers, and helped his mom cook dinner. There isn't much scripture that talks about his upbringing, but I would like to think that it was somewhat normal.

There is one story from his childhood found in Luke chapter 2. It's the story of the time that he ran away. Well, he kind of ran away. The story goes that Jesus and his family went to Jerusalem every year to observe the Feast of the Passover, which is a celebration in remembrance of the Passover in the Old Testament when God saved the Israelite people. When the party was over Jesus' family decided to go back home, but Jesus stayed in Jerusalem. Now I don't claim to be the best parent in the world, but I think that I would notice if my son was gone. The scriptures tell us that Mary and Joseph were not aware that Jesus was gone for a whole day's journey. On top of that, it took them three days to find him! After going all the way back to Jerusalem, they finally found Jesus in the Jewish temple sitting among the teachers, listening to them and asking questions.

Now, let's pause the story for a moment. Think about how abnormal this situation is. There is a 12-year-old boy who is without his parents in an unfamiliar city. Do you think that he found and paid for a hotel all on his own? Do you think he stayed with a family member or a stranger, or did he just sleep on the street? Did he at least have money for food? I'm not sure about you, but I have so many questions.

There is one scenario in this story that baffles me the most. In verses 46 and 47 it says, *"After three days they found him in the temple, sitting among the teachers, listening to them and asking them questions. And all who heard him were amazed at his understanding and his answers."*[3] So, you're telling me that there was a group of Jewish teachers who allowed a young boy to sit in on their teachings, and even participate by asking questions? Not only this, but the teachers were asking *him* questions as well? Could it be that even the teachers were learning from this 12-year-old Jesus? It says that they were *"amazed at his understanding and his answers."*[4] This is such an unbelievable story to me because throughout the Bible, we see all of the religious teachers and leaders as very prideful people who would not listen to anybody, much less a young boy. Sure, it's standard for boys around this age to start their own Rabbi training, but it still would have been inappropriate and out of the ordinary for him to have such authority. This just goes to show that Jesus was not normal. Even as a child, Jesus was different.

Now, Jesus continued to be different throughout his life, especially when he began his ministry. He was not in the slightest bit predictable. He was too different. There are some core differences in Jesus that we simply cannot replicate. The first of those differences was that Jesus was sinless. Can you imagine someone being sinless? If you're someone who was bothered by the seemingly-perfect kid in school, then you probably wouldn't have liked Jesus either. He was perfect in every way, and people hated him for it. We, on the other hand, are sinful; being sinless is a kind of different that we cannot attain.

Another big difference between Jesus and you and

me is that Jesus claimed to be and was the Son of God. Not merely a child of God and not one of God's unique creations, but the begotten Son of God. The word begotten is an English translation of the Greek word *monogenes,* which means *"pertaining to being the only one of its kind or class, unique in kind."*[5] Jesus was not just a child of God, he was the unique one of a kind Son of the living God.

Lastly, let's address the main difference: Jesus was fully God. I once heard my friend Aidan refer to Jesus as "God in a bod." [6] I think he was onto something. While Jesus was fully human, at the same time he was fully God. This is another difference that we could never achieve. But my goal is not to talk about these kinds of obvious differences; I want to talk about the abnormally different things Jesus did that we *can* attain.

Jesus did some pretty weird and unpredictable things throughout his ministry. Things like spitting in the dirt to make mud to rub on a blind man's eyes and heal him. Who could have predicted that? The Jewish people thought that the Messiah would be a domineering King on a stallion, but he was a humble carpenter on a donkey from Nazareth, spitting in dirt from time to time. During his ministry, Jesus even said that he was homeless. So when I say that Jesus was different, I mean he was *very* different. He was so different that many of us would have chosen not to follow him. Over the course of this book, we'll go over some very polarizing things that Jesus said and did. We will get to those stories soon, but first let's get a good grasp on the fact that Jesus was different, and then we can look at our own lives and see if we, too, are living differently.

I want you to hear this: BEING DIFFERENT ISN'T A BAD THING! Sure, it *can* be a bad thing, but it isn't always. Being unique is usually what leaders look like;

it's what makes them stand out. To be different like Jesus is in fact the best thing. As we journey together in this book, I want you to see how Jesus was different and even weird at times. He stood out, but not in a prideful way. He was counter-cultural, counter-religious, and counter-traditional. Jesus was very punk rock in the way that he did things. Just read the sermon on the mount––it's full of him sticking it to the man. Jesus says things like "You have heard this. Well, I tell you to do it differently." He challenges not only our actions but our intentions. He wants our lives to be different all the way to the core. He wants our thoughts to be different. He wants our reactions to situations to be different. He even wants our demeanor to be different. We are going to look at the life that Jesus lived, as well as the things that he taught, in order to learn from him and hopefully shape our lives into a life that looks more like Christ Jesus––a life that looks different.

I really want to press into what God wants for us. In order to do this, I am praying this incredible prayer that Moses prayed in Exodus 33:13:

> *"Now therefore, if I have found favor in your sight, please show me now your ways, that I may know you in order to find favor in your sight. Consider too that this nation is your people."*[7]

This is my prayer.

> *"Lord, I want to know you. I want to know your heart. I want to do what you will, so please show me your ways. I don't want the ways of the world, I don't want my ways, I want your ways. I want to know YOU! I want to know you more than anything. The*

*more that I know you, the more I can walk in
your ways and find favor in your sight."*

Don't you want to know God and find favor in his sight? Don't you want to be like Moses and have God speak to you as a man speaks to his friend? (Exodus 33:11) I want this so badly, both for you and me. I want to get to the end of my life to hear the joyful sound of my God saying, *"Well done, my good and faithful servant."*[8] So let's pray that God will show us his ways that we might know him.

In the book of Romans, the apostle Paul teaches us an important truth that I believe we need to grasp if we are going to live a life that is holy and acceptable to God. He says in chapter 12,

"I appeal to you therefore, brothers, by the mercies of God, to present your bodies as a living sacrifice, holy and acceptable to God, which is your spiritual worship. Do not be conformed to this world but be transformed by the renewal of your mind, that by testing you may discern what is the will of God, what is good and acceptable and perfect." [9]

There are a lot of things that we are being molded and conformed to that are *of this world*. The world is fighting for your attention, affection, and devotion; and believe it or not, the world has been winning some battles. Every ad that you see is telling you something. "You need to have *this*. You should be more like *that*." Or, "If only you were *here*, then you would be happy." But all of these messages are lies. The unfortunate reality is that we believe the lies that the world is giving us. We may not admit that we have fallen into the temptations of the world, but we have. I am not saying we have placed our faith in the world, but we have lost some battles in our fight against the world.

One of the most sobering verses in scripture is found

in Mark 8:36: *"For what does it profit a man to gain the whole world and forfeit his soul?"* [10] The world will offer anything and everything to you in exchange for your soul. The world will not use this exact verbiage, but in reality this is the deal that the world is proposing and it always over promises and under delivers. We might even be doing things that are considered "normal" in the church, but that are counter to what Jesus calls us to do. In order for us to become more like Jesus, we must renew our minds to think, see, and act the way Jesus would. This will be different. There may be things that we are doing that Jesus wants us to change. In these situations, we need to have a clear mind and a heart that is open to change.

Let's agree to be honest with ourselves and with God as we read the truths of his word and analyze if there are things in our lives that need to change in order to live like Jesus. This will be challenging, but I fully believe that if we make these changes in our lives, we will be transformed from the inside out.

Verse 3 in Romans chapter 12 says,

> *"For by the grace given to me I say to everyone among you not to think of himself more highly than he ought to think, but to think with sober judgment, each according to the measure of faith that God has assigned."* [11]

At the end of every chapter in this book there will be a few questions meant to be used as a self-assessment. As you read these questions, don't think about your answers regarding your friends, family, or pastor; think of yourself. This is very important, because you can't change others, but you *can* change yourself. You also should not ask others to make a change until you can properly exemplify the change yourself. So, draw a circle around you and ask the assessment questions to all of the people inside that circle. As you do this, remember what Paul says: "Don't think of yourself higher than you ought, but make a sober judgment." [12] Be honest. Be vulnerable. Do yourself a favor and be real. There is no use in lying to yourself or to God. I know that this can be hard, but I am not asking you to go confess all of your failures to the church next Sunday. I am just urging you to not waste this great opportunity for God to mold you.

2 Corinthians 13:5 says, *"Examine yourselves, to see whether you are in the faith. Test yourselves."* [13] This is exactly what we are doing—examining our lives against what the Bible says to see if we are living as God calls us to. If we fail the test, then we must make the necessary changes. This could mean adding thoughts, actions, or behaviors into our lives, or it could mean removing some of them from our lives. Either way, changes must be made. I know that you are not perfect. King Solomon said, *"The wisdom of the prudent is to give thought to their ways, but the folly of fools is deception."* [14] Don't deceive yourself and be a fool. Give thought to your ways and make a pure assessment. I believe that as you read these self-assessment questions at the end of the chapters, God will speak to you. Listen to God's voice. Please. I beg you. As it is said in scripture, *"Today, if you hear his voice, do not harden your hearts as in the rebellion."* [15] Open your heart to what God has for you. If you hear his voice while reading this book, trust that he has the best intentions for you and your life.

1. Are you afraid of judgment from others for being different for the sake of Jesus?
2. Are you open to making changes in your life in order to live like Jesus?

CHAPTER 2

The Worst Quote Ever

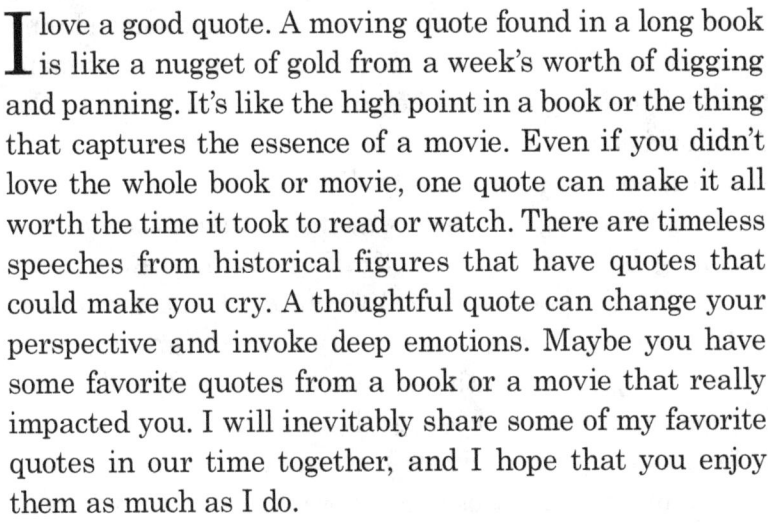

I love a good quote. A moving quote found in a long book is like a nugget of gold from a week's worth of digging and panning. It's like the high point in a book or the thing that captures the essence of a movie. Even if you didn't love the whole book or movie, one quote can make it all worth the time it took to read or watch. There are timeless speeches from historical figures that have quotes that could make you cry. A thoughtful quote can change your perspective and invoke deep emotions. Maybe you have some favorite quotes from a book or a movie that really impacted you. I will inevitably share some of my favorite quotes in our time together, and I hope that you enjoy them as much as I do.

I know, now you're probably hoping for a good quote. I'm actually going to share with you what is, in my opinion, the worst quote ever. Before I do, here is a great one that we can ponder on for a bit, and I will tie it into this chapter's theme.

> *"Ignoring isn't the same as ignorance,
> you have to work at it."*
> —Margaret Atwood, *The Handmaid's Tale*[16]

That quote is so true! And honestly, convicting. Don't you love it when a quote is so thought-provoking? There is a huge difference between the words *ignorance* and *ignore*. Although they sound the same, they are on the opposite ends of the spectrum. Ignorance is defined by Merriam-Webster's dictionary as a "lack of knowledge, education, or awareness." [17] This ultimately means that ignorance isn't really the fault of the person who is ignorant. He that is ignorant is just lacking the necessary knowledge to make the right decision. Let's be honest, we have all been ignorant to things before. When you were educated on what you were ignorant to, you probably felt some shame as a result. You may have also felt a bit of enlightenment though because you were then aware and able to make the right decision.

To ignore is a completely different thing. When you ignore something, you are refusing to take notice of it.[18] Ignoring is declining, rejecting, or turning away from the truth. Do you see the difference? While ignorance is literally not being aware of the truth, ignoring is a choice to reject the truth when we know it fully well. Let's be honest, we've all been guilty of ignoring something before. For instance, when I see a "No Skateboarding" sign, I often just choose to ignore it. I am fully aware that skateboarding is prohibited because of the sign, but I refuse, decline, reject, or turn away from that truth. Why?

Well, it's because I want my own way. I care more about my will than the will of others—namely, whoever posted the "No Skateboarding" sign.

This is what it all boils down to: at its purest form, ignoring is selfishness. Acts 17:30 says, "The times of ignorance God overlooked, but now he commands all people everywhere to repent." What an amazing God we serve, that he would overlook our ignorance. How many times have we wished that people would overlook our ignorance? Or, how many times do we judge and condemn other people who are ignorant? Are there any parents out there who have learned the art of overlooking and forgiving what your toddler did in their ignorance? I'm still learning that one. But God is so rich in grace and mercy that he looks past our ignorance! Now *that* is a loving Father who is slow to anger towards his ignorant children.

Now, let's get back to the worst quote ever. It is a fairly well-known quote that I absolutely despise. I am *not* ignorant to the fact that this quote might be one that you love and often use. So if this is one of your favorite quotes, I'm sorry to burst your bubble. Just know that I am sharing this out of love—love for Jesus and love for his people. Here goes nothing. *"Preach the gospel at all times, and when necessary, use words."*

Phew, we made it! Now, this might be something that you are ignorant of. Maybe you have no idea that this is a truth in scripture, and that's okay; we'll unpack it. On the other hand, this might be something that you are totally aware of and may or may not be ignoring. This quote has formerly been attributed to St. Francis of Assisi, but this has never been confirmed. I personally don't think that he would have said such a thing because of his theology and the way that he lived. Actually, I think he would majorly disapprove of this quote. At face value, it sounds much better than it actually is. A first glance might tell you that this is an incredibly insightful quote. There's no telling how many times I've read this quote in books or heard it used in sermons or conferences. Every time I hear it, I cringe and pray for the ignorance of the person sharing the quote.

I will say that I love the first portion of this quote. *"Preach the gospel at all times."* Yes and amen! Do you know anyone who is like this? Someone who simply cannot stop talking about the good news that Jesus died for our sins and conquered sin and death forever? I know some people like that and I envy them in a way. Sure, some of them are a bit wild or weird, but I admire them. There is one guy that comes to mind, and maybe you have heard of him. His name is Mike Servin. If you haven't heard of him, just give him a quick google or look him up on social media. You will quickly find that this guy cannot stop talking about Jesus. He literally goes around yelling, "Jesus Christ, I love you God!" This guy is someone who I think of when I hear *"preach the gospel at all times."* I want us all to be people who embody and exude the idea of preaching the gospel at all times.

Now for the second portion of the quote. Ugh... I will fight tooth and nail over this part because it's heinous: *"... and when necessary, use words."* Before you attack me, I fully understand that the complete quote is implying that Christ followers should live a life that exemplifies Jesus at all times. I also believe and agree with this truth. In fact, I believe it so strongly that I decided to write this whole book about how Jesus lived and how we can live just like him! I am pro living like Christ and showing the gospel by the way that we live.

Think back to the question I asked earlier about people who share the gospel at all times: *"Do you know anyone who is like this? Someone who simply cannot stop talking about the good news that Jesus died for our sins and conquered sin and death forever?"* Now I want to ask a similar question. Do you know anyone who loves people like Jesus, is humble like Jesus, forgives like Jesus, is kind like Jesus, is compassionate like Jesus, generous, faithful, gentle, caring, patient, and all of the other characteristics of Jesus, *but* they are not a Christian? I do. Some of the most decent people I have ever met are not Christians. They live lives that look more like Jesus than some actual followers of Jesus that I know. But they don't believe the gospel. This is quite unfortunate. Imagine asking that person to give an account for why they live such a life. Do you think that they will answer by explaining the good news of Jesus? No chance—they don't know the good news. Even if they do know it, they don't believe it.

One last question on this: do you know anyone who lives a life that exemplifies Jesus and the gospel, but they don't evangelize? I'm sure that you do. Well, if I was a betting man, I would have pretty good odds to wager that your own name was the first name that popped into your head. You're not alone. Less than 5% of Christians share the gospel with one person per year.[19] I think it would be a safe bet that you might be in the 95% of Christians who do not share the gospel with even a single person every year. If you are in the 5%, kudos to you; but this is only an example of sharing the gospel with *one* person per year. This is not even close to preaching the gospel *"at all times."* If you are in the 95%, I am not trying to make you feel bad. I want us to assess where we stand. Are we in the 95% or are we *different*?

My opinion honestly isn't worth much, so let's look at what the inspired and infallible Word of God says. Paul brings us a beautiful truth in Romans 10. Yeah, we are going straight to the passage that will destroy this quote from the get-go. *"How then will they call on him in whom they have not believed? And how are they to believe in him of whom they have never heard? And how are they to hear without someone preaching?" (Romans 10:14)*[20]

I like that Paul works from back to front in this scenario: call, believe, hear, and preach. It's like he wants to show us that the goal of them calling on the Lord can only happen if and when these other things first take place. So let's look at this in the reverse sequence that Paul writes in order for us to see it from an evangelistic perspective.

As Christ followers, we are first called to preach. This word *preach* in scripture really means to proclaim or herald the good news with your words. The first step is to use our words to verbally and vocally share the good news of Jesus. This alone gives us an understanding that our words are always "necessary." Still don't believe me? Okay, imagine this scenario. Put yourself in this story. You personally are living the most Christ-like life that you could ever imagine. You exemplify Jesus so well that anyone who looks at you could tell that there is something very special about the way you live. Now a stranger approaches you and gives you the greatest setup question to share the gospel ever by saying, "Hello there, I noticed that you live life in such a different way. It's so attractive, but I cannot pinpoint why that is. Could you explain your reasoning for why you live life the way that you do?"

This is the dream scenario, right? I pray to God that he would grace me with someone who pitches me this perfect evangelistic setup just to knock it out of the park. Again, put yourself in this situation and imagine what your response would be. I think we'd all agree that this would be the opportune time to gladly use your words and share the good news of Jesus: that true hope is found in him alone and that he is the reason for the way you live your life. Am I Right?

But imagine that you firmly believe the words of this quote. Is this the only necessary time to share the gospel? Where is the line? How can you tell when it is a necessary time to use words to share the gospel? Is there ever a bad time to share the gospel using words? I will agree that there is wisdom to discerning when and where we share the gospel, but there is always a necessity in using words when sharing the gospel. Joel Tiegreen, a missionary to Turkey, once said, "I understand, don't be a fool. Getting a megaphone in Saudi Arabia and going in front of a mosque, it will be your last, I'm sure. But then, I wouldn't say that you shouldn't do that, but it's probably a bad idea. But never sharing the gospel with someone until you know them for two or three years is ridiculous. You can't live in fear like that, you should share the gospel with as many people as you can, and if bad things happen to you because you're sharing the gospel, then bad things happen because you were being obedient, and that is not something to be ashamed of." [21]

Back to the dream scenario—what if you decided to not give an answer at all and just let your actions speak for themselves? To be honest, most people would give a vague answer to that person by saying something like, "Oh, thanks for noticing, I am just a really good and decent person," or, "Well, my parents raised me to be loving and kind so I guess that you can attribute the life that I live to my amazing parents." Or people might just be humble and say, "I'm okay, but I'm not that great." None of these would be a good response. I would go as far to say that any of these responses would be a complete and utter failure and a wasted opportunity to share the best news ever and glorify God in the process.

The Bible says in 1 Peter 3:15, *"But in your hearts honor Christ the Lord as holy, always being prepared to make a defense to anyone who asks you for a reason for the hope that is in you; yet do it with gentleness and respect."*[22] I believe that God is reminding us to be ready and prepared at all times, and to use our words to share the gospel. This doesn't mean that you have to have a script for when the time comes, but it does mean that we should always be willing and able to share our faith with others.

Some of you might be wondering how you'd respond in this situation. Maybe you don't feel equipped to share the gospel. Maybe you feel a sense of fear at the very thought of sharing your faith. Perhaps you don't think that God is "calling you" to share your faith. At the very least, most of you would love to give a good response, even if you are fearful or do not know what you would say. Well, let me try to put your mind and heart at ease.

First, if you believe and understand the good news of Jesus yourself, then you can at least share the foundational principles of the gospel. You don't have to have a master's degree in theology or be a pastor in order to explain the basics of the gospel. Secondly, you have nothing to fear. If you trust in Jesus as your Savior, you have the Holy Spirit of God himself dwelling inside you. Scripture promises that the Spirit will be with you always. Even more so, the Bible tells us in Luke 12:12, *"for the Holy Spirit will teach you in that very hour what you ought to say."*[23] This should be a great comfort for us, especially when sharing our faith. Lastly, evangelism might not be your spiritual gift. I get it. I am also not gifted with a love or talent of changing diapers, but this does not exempt me from doing so. Evangelism is a way for you to serve God's people as a benefit to them and as you do this, God will build your faith. You have the honor and privilege to be the person that gives someone the good news of Jesus' redeeming love! Their life is full of sin and death, and *you* get to be the one to offer them a new life with Jesus that takes away that sin and brings them back into a relationship with their Father and God who loves them. The Bible is full of commands for us to preach the gospel to all creation. This is not a command to a limited few, but for every single follower of Christ.

You might be thinking, "Well Brooks, that's easier said than done." I would have to say that, yes, I agree. That is why I want to share with you a possible response that you could give someone. Like 1 Peter says, we can and should prepare for this situation.[24] Today it's hypothetical, but even tomorrow could be the real deal. This response comes directly from scripture. In Galatians 2:20 Paul says, *"I have been crucified with Christ. It is no longer I who live, but Christ who lives in me. And the life I now live in the flesh I live by faith in the Son of God, who loved me and gave himself for me."*[25]

Imagine the follow up questions that you could receive from a response like this. Now I know that this could be confusing for them, which is why I would suggest that you use this verse as a template of sorts. You could even change the wording a bit to be less confusing to the listener that you are speaking to. I think that this is important because we don't want to confuse people from the beginning. So instead of directly quoting this scripture verse, maybe you could say something like this: "Wow, thanks for noticing. I wasn't always this way, in fact I used to be a totally different person. You know, my life used to be quite sad and hopeless. It wasn't until I put my faith in Jesus that my life began to change. I used to live for myself and that wasn't working. When someone shared with me the truth that Jesus gave up his life to pay for my sins, I started to seek out what that meant. Finally, after searching and praying, I decided to give up my way of life to live for Jesus. Now the life that I live, for God and others, represents the love that Jesus has for me." At this point, we simply wait for their response––and there *will* be a response. We have been obedient to share the good news with our words, and I believe that the Lord finds joy in our obedience.

I need you to know something important. This scenario doesn't always end the way you hope it will. In fact, you can almost expect the opposite. But you cannot share the gospel with fear of what may or may not happen. We share the gospel because of two main reasons. First is out of our love for God. We should be overflowing with love because this good news is not just something that we share, it is something that we have obtained. This good news is ours and we should be so in love with our God who has given us this good news through Jesus that we can't help but share it. Secondly, we should share the gospel out of our love for God's people. You know, the ones that Jesus died for, just like you and me. There are 7.9 billion people in the world, many of whom have never heard the name of Jesus. This makes me extremely sad. It burdens me. I am literally tearing up at the thought as I write this. Like Jesus, when he looked out on a crowd, he was moved with compassion because they looked *"harassed and helpless, like sheep without a shepherd."*[26] Every unbeliever in the world looks this way to Jesus. Think about that. Every single person who has not put their faith in Jesus is harassed by Satan and is completely and utterly helpless in their sin on their own. We have a choice to love them like Jesus does and share the gospel with them, or pass them by with a lack of compassion. Think of the person, or even the countless people, who shared the gospel with you. I am so thankful for all of the people who were loving and bold enough to share the gospel with me, because if it were not for them, I don't know where else I would have heard the good news of Jesus.

To conclude the Romans equation, if we preach, they will hear. This is our role, and it is the only part of the equation that we have control over. If we share the gospel, then we have given people the chance to hear, believe, and call on the Lord for salvation. Jesus was different because he did not simply live a perfect life, he preached the good news. He was vocal to tell people that he was there as the Messiah to bring salvation to the world.

One of my favorite moments from Jesus in scripture is found in Luke chapter 4. Jesus goes to his hometown of Nazareth, and on the Sabbath he goes to the synagogue like he normally would, but this time to preach. Jesus does one of the most incredible and bold things that anyone could ever do. He stands up and reads a passage of scripture from the prophet Isaiah that says, *"The Spirit of the Lord is upon me, because he has anointed me to proclaim good news to the poor. He has sent me to proclaim liberty to the captives and recovering of sight to the blind to set at liberty those who are oppressed, to proclaim the year of the Lord's favor."*[27] At this point Jesus rolls up the scroll and delivers the biggest mic drop in history by saying, *"Today this Scripture has been fulfilled in your hearing."*[28] Jesus made it known that he was the Messiah, and the good news was that he was there to fulfill the prophecies that they had been waiting for. He specifically said that he was there to proclaim good news, and he would continue to do this throughout his ministry. At the very beginning of Jesus' ministry, it is recorded in Matthew 4 that *"From that time Jesus began to preach, saying, "Repent, for the kingdom of heaven is at hand."*[29] Whether it was for the Gentiles to know the good news, from creation all the way to eternity, or for the Jewish people to know that the Messiah had come, fulfilling all of the prophecies, Jesus knew that it was imperative for people to hear the good news of the gospel spoken to them.

If it were not necessary for us to use words when sharing the gospel, then Jesus would not have set the example, or given us the command to share the gospel with our words. It is plain and simple that it is more than necessary. Let's remember to obey this call from God to always share the gospel with all creation––both with our lives *and* our words. So, be like Jesus. Be different. Use your words.

*"Preach the gospel at all times,
and at* all *times use words."*

1. What is the main thing holding you back from sharing the gospel? Name it.
2. Pray and ask God to reveal three people that you should share the gospel with.
3. Now that you are not ignorant to this truth, are you willing to put this into practice this week? Why not reach out to one of the above people right now through call, text, or email?

CHAPTER 3

Is It Cake?

It's no secret that Jesus ruffled some feathers. People had all kinds of qualms about Jesus regarding everything from his actions to his words. But, Jesus spoke the truth. I don't mean some partial and surface level truth; no, he spoke deep-rooted truth that would sometimes surprise people. Jesus spoke truth about the seen and the unseen, the physical and the spiritual. He gripped the hearts of man with his words and he was unapologetic for it. People would travel from all over to listen to Jesus speak because he spoke with truth and authority.

Jesus spoke to many people, but he had two major audiences: the Jews and the Gentiles. In biblical times, the Gentiles were non-Jewish people who typically believed in a god or gods of some sort, but they didn't exactly believe that the God of the Jews, as talked about in the Torah, was the God of the universe. The Gentiles were also not Jewish by blood. The Jewish people, on the other hand, were Hebrew people—you know, descendants of Abraham. These were Jesus' chosen people, his family, and his religious brethren. Ironically, the Jewish people were the ones that Jesus offended the most. They were always on guard around Jesus, either defending themselves or trying to catch him in a trap and use his words against him. Besides the fact that he claimed to be and was the son of God, Jesus challenged their ways of life, and even more so, their hearts. The Jewish people were the ones that were looking forward to the Messiah coming, but many of them didn't accept Jesus as their long-awaited Savior.

Jesus' main targets were the Pharisees. These guys were the religious leaders and teachers of a large sect of the Jewish people and were held in very high esteem in the Jewish community. You could say that they were the big shots. These guys were very strict about the law, which is odd because they tended to add onto the law their traditional ways of life. Jesus cared deeply for these people, so much so that he decided to share the truth with them when they were in the wrong. Again, he would do this out of immense love for them and love for the people that they were teaching. Jesus wanted them to have the heart of God, and he saw some things that didn't seem right.

Have you ever questioned or challenged someone? Maybe this person said something that you knew was wrong, or maybe even a point-blank lie. I feel like it's hard to confront someone when we are in this situation. Let's be honest, most of us don't like confrontation. Now imagine that you are in this exact situation, but it's not just anyone, it's your pastor. How hard would it be to confront them about what they said? Or, what if it wasn't something they said, but something they did? Let's say he told the congregation on Sunday not to gossip, and then you heard him gossip about the church staff the following Monday. Would you call him out on it?

This is the situation that Jesus often found himself in with the Pharisees. This was not a one-time occurrence either; it happened all the time. There is actually a portion of scripture that is referred to as the "Woes of the Pharisees." This is just a chunk of scripture where Jesus rebukes, criticizes, and warns the Pharisees over and over again. If you were a Pharisee listening to these chapters, you were definitely embarrassed and most likely upset at Jesus.

There's a show on Netflix that has been in the top 10 on my feed lately called *"Is It Cake?"*[30] If you haven't seen it, this show is pretty incredible. It's also a fairly appropriate show, which is hard to find these days. The premise of the show is this: there are contestants who are extremely good at art. These people bake and decorate cakes that turn out looking nothing like cake. The cakes that they bake resemble physical objects. It could be an inanimate object; a bowling ball for instance, a hat, or toilet paper. Or, it could be in the likeness of another food, like a cheeseburger. These people are so good at making cake look like something else that they can place their finished cake side by side with the actual object and the judges cannot tell which one is cake and which one is real. As you watch, you try to guess which one *you* think is the cake. This show just exemplifies how easy it can be to fool people into believing that something is true when in actuality, it is false. The truth is, you don't really know until you see the inside. As they say, the proof is in the pudding.

The big reveal is when the show host takes a big knife

and attempts to cut into the object that is thought to be the cake. It is at this moment that we find out if the object is truly what it is portraying, or if it is a sham, a phony, a lie.

Of course, in this show, when you sniff out the lie you feel happy and accomplished, because it's only cake. But what about when we find out that someone we know is a phony? We are usually appalled and feel deceived and hurt, because it hurts to be lied to. Jesus would have been great at this show, because he can't be fooled. He sees right through the phony, and ultimately, he's hurt by it. Jesus knows that it is not the outside, but the inside that shows the truth. The outside can be fabricated and deceiving, but the truth is found on the inside.

Jesus spoke to this truth often, because even his conversation topics were different. It was something that grieved him, and unlike the average human, he wasn't afraid of confrontation. In the book of Matthew, Jesus speaks to this exact issue. You see, the Pharisees were having a problem with presenting an appearance of being godly. Not that it's a problem to be godly, this would be ideal. The problem would be giving a false appearance of godliness, and this is where the Pharisees stood. Everyone looked up to them because they looked like they had it all figured out. They were following the law, they dressed up in holy attire, and they taught the law with zeal; but on the inside, they were living a lie.

We find our passage in Matthew chapter 23 verses 27-28. It says, *"Woe to you, scribes and Pharisees, hypocrites! For you are like whitewashed tombs, which outwardly appear beautiful, but within are full of dead people's bones and all uncleanness. So you also outwardly appear righteous to others, but within you are full of hypocrisy and lawlessness."*[31]

On the inside, in their hearts, the Pharisees were

the opposite of what they showed on the outside. They appeared to be righteous and lawful. To the eye, they seemed like they had it all put together. But in reality they were hypocrites and living a lie. Jesus spoke directly to them and said, *you're not fooling me!* The hardest part for the Pharisees was that in their hearts, they knew that it was true. Hypocrites know their condition, but it is hard to change. Jesus says in another passage that the Pharisees have received their reward. We find this in Matthew chapter 6 where Jesus says, *"Thus, when you give to the needy, sound no trumpet before you, as the hypocrites do in the synagogues and in the streets, that they may be praised by others. Truly, I say to you, they have received their reward."*[32] The reward that the hypocrites would receive is the praise from others. They have fooled the people and the people have in return given them praise that they do not deserve. This is their reward, nothing more.

Jesus commands us to do things differently, *"But when you give to the needy, do not let your left hand know what your right hand is doing, so that your giving may be in secret. And your Father who sees in secret will reward you."*[33] Jesus is giving us a better way. You might not be seen and praised by others, but you will be seen and rewarded by God himself!

This reminds me of a video that I watched one time of a magician. This magician would perform his magic tricks and wow the onlookers, only for someone watching to yell out the secret of the trick, thus exposing the magician. Well, the first time this happened the magician quickly diverted the attention of everyone to, you guessed it, another trick. He goes back to his comfort zone of trickery that is falsely believed to be *"magic."* Again, he continues to set up his trick, but this time the onlooker gives the crowd a play-by-play. He walks the crowd through the trickery in real time. As you can imagine, the magician is not happy. He is exposed and laid bare before the audience as a mere, mortal human.

I would not advise doing this; in fact, this onlooker was kind of a jerk. But this analogy still resonates with our story. The magician was used to fooling people with his tricks. He did not want his secret to be revealed. No one wants to be exposed as a lie or a phony. So think about the Pharisees––they were being exposed as hypocrites. Even the onlookers couldn't see the lie, but Jesus could and he was calling it out. In the same way that the onlookers didn't see the tricks of the magician, but that one person could.

Now, does this mean that we are not to trust anyone? Should we never listen to any pastors and teachers ever again for fear of them being hypocrites and false teachers? Slow down––I am very hopeful that your pastor can be trusted. There are false teachers out there, yes, but let's not get overwhelmed by this thought. There might be times when we are being fooled, but how are we supposed to know if we are being deceived? Luckily, Jesus tells us what to look for when trying to recognize false teachers in the Sermon on the Mount. He says, *"Beware of false prophets, who come to you in sheep's clothing but inwardly are ravenous wolves. You will recognize them by their fruits. Are grapes gathered from thorn bushes, or figs from thistles? So, every healthy tree bears good fruit, but the diseased tree bears bad fruit. A healthy tree cannot bear bad fruit, nor can a diseased tree bear good fruit. Every tree that does not bear good fruit is cut down and thrown into the fire. Thus you will recognize them by their fruits."*[34]

This passage is packed with good teaching for us. First, we just need to beware, or be aware. So many believers

Is It Cake?

are unaware that there are teachers out there who are leading people astray. They say that ignorance is bliss, but it's not. Do you know what the definition of bliss is? Webster defines bliss as "complete happiness, paradise, heaven."[35] Who in their right mind would ever think that being ignorant is equal to heaven? No one.

So, I want us all to be aware that there are people, even in the church, that could be a wolf in sheep's clothing. This is saying that these people will look like harmless sheep at face value. They will probably seem like followers of Jesus, but they are not. My mind quickly goes to Judas. He was one of the twelve OG's. How could it be that Judas was going to betray Jesus? This is one of the biggest plot twists in the history of the world. I am not saying they are in your church, I'm just saying they are out there. Now, let's not go on some wild hunt here. I certainly do not advise making any accusations right now. There is a nicely laid out process in the Bible of accountability and church discipline, and no one is above church discipline.

So how can we tell if someone is who they say they are? We have to look at their life––the whole thing. Jesus doesn't just see the face value, he sees and tests all by the trial of life over time. You might be able to tell that someone could be leading people astray by observing a pattern of them doing things that are unbiblical. There is a reason that Paul reminds us in the Bible to search the scriptures to see if his teachings are true. We should do the same with anyone who we are gleaning from spiritually. Let's be sure that they are teaching from the Bible.

Here are some practical questions that you can ask: What are they producing? What are the fruits of their labor? Can you see the fruit of the Spirit in them? Are they living a spirit-filled life that looks, sounds, and feels like Jesus? Are they glorifying God in their everyday life?

Are they obeying the commands of Christ? Do they make disciples of Jesus? Do they practice what they preach?

Please know that this does not mean that everyone outside of perfection is a wolf or a false prophet. We all fall short of God's glory. We all have times that we fail. Even your pastors and spiritual leaders will fail, but this does not mean that they are a wolf trying to lead you astray.

Maybe we are looking at this from only one vantage point. So far we have been looking from the point of view of the onlookers, but what if we put ourselves in the Pharisee's sandals? Maybe you are a pastor, ministry worker, small group leader, or disciple-maker. I think we need to look at ourselves and ask, *what does my life produce?* Am I representing Christ and bearing the fruit of the Spirit? Am I being a hypocrite in some areas in my walk with Jesus? I am sure that when we are honest with ourselves, we will find things that are hypocritical.

So what does all of this have to do with Jesus? Jesus was different in the way that he was not a hypocrite. He practiced what he preached. There was never a time that he stepped outside of the bounds of God's law. 1 Peter 2:22 says, *"He committed no sin, neither was deceit found in his mouth."*[36] Jesus was perfect, and there was no deceit in him. He did not deceive the people as the Pharisees did; he was truthful in his words and deeds. Hebrews 4:15 says, *"For we do not have a high priest who is unable to sympathize with our weaknesses, but one who in every respect has been tempted as we are, yet without sin."*[37] Jesus was tempted to do exactly what the Pharisees were doing, but still was without sin. Have you ever thought about this? Jesus was tempted to have the outward appearance of righteousness while on the inside being a phony. But Jesus chose to be honest in his doing, to have pure motives, and to be the perfect example of life and godliness.

Jesus also was different in the way that he approached this issue. He didn't like hypocrisy, especially when it was coming from teachers and those in leadership. He was willing to call people out for their hypocrisy. This took some honesty and willingness to engage in a potentially uncomfortable situation. This wasn't something that Jesus did just for kicks, and I really don't think that he looked forward to this, but he knew when it was necessary. We also need to use wisdom to know when it is appropriate to address this with those who are living a hypocritical life claiming to live for Jesus. James 5:20 says, *"Let him know that whoever brings back a sinner from his wandering will save his soul from death and will cover a multitude of sins."*[38] We might have people in our lives that are beginning to live a hypocritical life posing to live for Jesus, and James says that we should bring that person back from their wandering away from him. In order to do this, we must be willing to have a potentially uncomfortable confrontation with them about their sin. We must remember that this must be done with love. Without love, our motives will be wrong. There is no other way we should approach someone about sin in their life. Even if it is because of zeal for the Lord Jesus, if we are lacking love for that person and their relationship with Jesus, our approach would be in vain.

God cares about the *why*. Why do we do the things we do? Why do we serve, give, teach, or share? The truth is, we all have things that we need to work on. Are you serving just because you think that it's the right thing to do? Do you teach to be seen and heard? Do you give out of generosity or to feel good about yourself? Take some time to really think about your fruit and know that what scripture says in Hebrews is true: *"And no creature is hidden from his sight, but all are naked and exposed to the eyes of him to whom we must give account."*[39] We are all exposed to God. He sees our actions and our intentions. We cannot hide the truth from him. You might look like a devout follower of Christ on the outside, but God truly knows if you are really his follower, or if you're just cake.

1. What are three ways that you have been hypocritical or fake in your walk with Jesus?
2. What are three fruits of the Spirit that you see in you as an outcome of your walk with Jesus?
3. What is one change that you can make today? Pray for this change.

CHAPTER 4

Only the Servants Knew

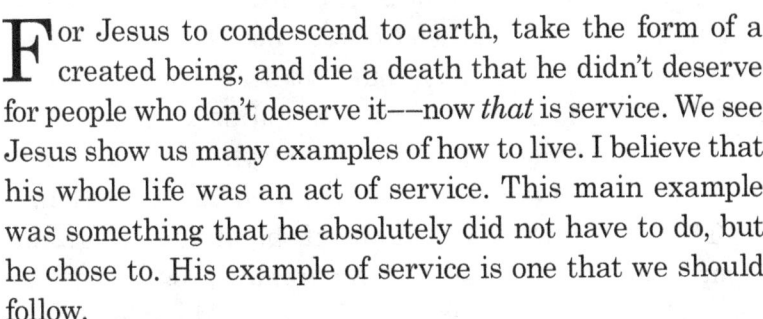

For Jesus to condescend to earth, take the form of a created being, and die a death that he didn't deserve for people who don't deserve it——now *that* is service. We see Jesus show us many examples of how to live. I believe that his whole life was an act of service. This main example was something that he absolutely did not have to do, but he chose to. His example of service is one that we should follow.

In this chapter we are going to be talking about serving one another and serving God. Serving is not always easy, but it is something that Jesus calls us to. Service is one of the attributes of Jesus that we need to investigate in order to see how he was different in his serving. In the next chapter we will look at a different perspective that is even more important, but we will get there later.

Don't we all just love to be acknowledged for our service? I know that I do. I don't think that it is a bad thing to acknowledge people for their service. I actually think that it is quite honorable to acknowledge people and give them a thank you for whatever they have done. Whenever I hear that someone served in our military, I quickly thank them for their service. I believe this is a good thing. What's *not* good is serving for the lone reason of being acknowledged. We should view acknowledgement as the cherry on top. Unfortunately, for many of us, acknowledgement is at least a major motivator in why we serve.

We also tend to serve only where we think we'd *like* serving. You know, where we are gifted or where we think is the most enjoyable. Well, I have some bad news for you: serving is not always fun. Even though you aren't *"gifted"* at manual labor, that might be the service opportunity with the most need. Come to think of it, most opportunities to serve are not particularly fun and they are usually things that take no skill or gifting. All that it requires is a willing servant. Charles Spurgeon says, "He who does not serve God where he is would not serve God anywhere else."[40] Many believe that they would serve if only the circumstances were different, but maybe God is asking us to serve right where we are in our current situation.

This makes me think of one of the annual programs at my church. We host a kids summer program called Sports Camp. Every year around April or May, the church announces that we are looking for volunteers for Sports Camp. It's a week-long venture for the kids to learn about Jesus and have some fun learning and playing sports, and we have hundreds of kids sign up every year to participate. To pull this off, we need as many volunteers as we can get. For weeks the pastors announce from stage that we are looking for volunteers and that they'll take anyone, regardless of skills or gifting; *we just need willing servants!* They usually give some line like, *ask not what Sports Camp can do for you, but what you can do for Sports Camp!*

I want to give you some context for this camp. We are in Southwest Florida and the temperatures will surely be in the high 90's and maybe even over 100 degrees in the summer. Humidity will be in the same number range as the temperature. You will be surrounded by hundreds of screaming children who will not listen to you. To make things worse, the kids will be eating candy and drinking soda every day. In the event of the high chance that it will rain, we will be stuck inside—*with* the hundreds of screaming kids. Again, the kids will not listen to you. We will most definitely be short on volunteers, so you will have to wear a lot of hats. You might have signed up to serve lunch, but I'm sorry, we actually need you to coach gymnastics. Oh, and this is strictly a volunteer role—there will be no pay. And I can't stress this enough: the kids will *not* listen to you.

This is often what serving looks like; knowing that it might not be glamorous, but that it's about serving others. In my opinion, blessed are the people who say yes to Sports Camp, for they are the true servants.

I want us to look at the story of Jesus' first recorded miracle when he turned water into wine. I know, that's quite the contrast from Sports Camp. This is a story that is well-known at face value, but it is rarely used for a deeper teaching about serving. I want to go deeper into this story with you. Trust me, I am just as amazed as you are that Jesus turned roughly 150 gallons of water into wine. I have never had *"good"* wine, and I am also pretty cheap. So I wouldn't think to spend no more than $10 on a bottle of wine. But I can only imagine that this was that top shelf, super expensive kind of wine. In fact, scripture says that the hosts of the party think it tastes even better than the first round of prepared wine.[41]

Regardless, the quantity or quality of the wine is not what we will be focusing on. I want us to look at the service portion of the miracle. Remember that Jesus was different, and he did things in a different way.

The story goes that Jesus and his disciples were invited to a wedding in Cana. The wedding was presumably going great; that is, until they ran out of wine. When the problem arose, Mary, the mother of Jesus, immediately brought the problem to Jesus and told him, *"They have no wine."*[42]

Can we first take this as a lesson in and of itself? When a problem arises in our life, let's take the approach of Mary and immediately bring it to Jesus. How often do we go straight to brainstorming a solution, phoning a friend, or asking chatGPT? Let's learn from Mary and go directly to Jesus.

So clearly, Mary has faith that Jesus would know how (and would be able) to fix their little wine dilemma. Jesus tries to tell his mom that it might not be the right time. What Jesus probably meant by this was that it was God that determined when his public earthly miracles would begin, not Mary. Nonetheless, Mary turned to the servants and said, *"Do whatever he tells you."*[43] Mary has some immense wisdom that is shown here. First she takes the problem to Jesus, and then she yields all plans to Jesus' will. Again, let's learn from Mary in this. How rare is it for us to go straight to Jesus to ask for wisdom and guidance? And how rare is it that we listen and do whatever he tells us to do? If we are honest with ourselves, this is probably not our default response.

Now, this is where the story starts to get weird. Jesus tells the servants to fill these huge jars full of water. This

Only the Servants Knew

wasn't some mason jar—when I say huge, I mean *20-30 gallons each* type of huge. Do you know the kind of work that it took to fill these water jars? It was hard work. Remember, there was no running water in Jesus' time. This means the servants had to go to a (hopefully) nearby well, fill a bucket of water, take this bucket back to the wedding venue, dump the bucket of water into one of these six massive jars, and then repeat the process. Again, this was an estimated 150 gallons of water. Imagine carrying a five gallon bucket of water 30 times from the well to the wedding venue. Jesus was not asking them to do something easy. These servants were also probably quite confused. Why would Jesus ask them to do all of this work? I can hear them now: *Uhh Jesus, we need wine, not water. Why are we doing this?* I would assume that the servants weren't even allowed to drink the wine. My guess would be that they were only there to serve.

The servants took Mary's advice though; they did whatever Jesus told them to do. They had trust and a faith that what Jesus was asking them to do was going to be worth it. So the servants worked hard, they took the trips back and forth, and they didn't complain. They didn't do a mediocre job either. The passage says that they filled the jars to the brim. This means they didn't stop when the jars looked "close enough"—they fully fulfilled their duties of filling the jars. Sometimes when we serve, we don't do a great job. Let's be honest, we usually think that because we are giving our time and energy at all, we don't have to serve at the highest level; we are already doing more than others, anyway. Am I wrong? This scripture shows us that Jesus expects more from us as we serve, even the best of our ability.

Imagine being the servants at this particular part of the story. They are probably tired, sweaty, and confused.

At this point, Jesus then asks them to draw some of the water out and take it to the master of the feast, AKA their boss. What's going through their minds? They are about to bring the boss a tall glass of water, and they know that it's water because they are the ones that filled the jars—with *water!* They were probably feeling a bit of fear, and rightfully so. Even though they knew that it was water, they did what Jesus told them to do and they took a cup to the master of the feast.

The pinnacle moment is here, when the master of the feast takes a sip. We all know his response as told in scripture. This is possibly the best wine that he has ever tasted. He is amazed because this wine was superior to the first wine that was served throughout the first half of the night. Not only was he amazed at the quality of the wine, but he was struck at the order in which the quality came. It was different.

Now scripture tells us that the master of the feast did not know where the wine had come from. This means that he had no idea that a miracle had taken place. For all that he knew, they just had another batch of wine waiting for this moment. He thought that they were holding out on him. He was completely unaware of the fullness of the situation, but do you know who was fully aware? The servants.

I can only imagine the look on their faces when they realized that it wasn't water that the master was drinking. In verse 9, it is written that it was known by the servants where the wine had come from, after also specifically saying that the master of the feast did not know.[44] For all we know, every single one of the wedding attendees were also oblivious to the fact that they were drinking wine that only moments ago was water. Only the servants knew.

Here is the big takeaway: it is the servants who see

the fullness of God's provision. Remember, everyone at the wedding benefited from the miracle, but only the servants knew that a miracle took place. The wedding guests and the master of the feast only saw in part, but the servants observed and experienced the fullness of what Jesus had for everyone in the situation. This passage goes on to say that this was the moment Jesus manifested his glory! These servants could have missed out on the manifestation of the glory of Jesus if they were unwilling to serve and work hard, or if they were not willing to trust Jesus when he asked them to do something that took a lot of faith.

Do you want to experience the fullness of what God has for you? Of course you do. That is not in question. The real question is, are you willing to serve in order to experience the fullness? We need to remind ourselves that when Jesus is the one asking us to serve, the right response is what Mary says: *"Do whatever he tells you."*

This is only one of the many examples of serving in the Bible. Of course, the best example of all is the example of Jesus' life and death. In Philippians 2, Paul and Timothy word it better than I ever could in saying, *"Do nothing from selfish ambition or conceit, but in humility count others more significant than yourselves. Let each of you look not only to his own interests, but also to the interests of others. Have this mind among yourselves, which is yours in Christ Jesus, who, though he was in the form of God, did not count equality with God a thing to be grasped, but emptied himself, by taking the form of a servant, being born in the likeness of men. And being found in human form, he humbled himself by becoming obedient to the point of death, even death on a cross."* [45]

See, you have the ability to think this way. Paul says this is yours in Christ Jesus. So why is it so hard for us to serve one another? It's hard enough for us to serve our fellow brothers and sisters in Christ, but how much harder is it for us to serve the ones who are directly opposed to us? There are times when it's hard to serve my wife––and I love her more than anyone in the world! The heart of the matter is that we are all selfish. We would rather be served than to serve. We feel like we deserve something, or *everything.*

The truth is that we don't really want what we deserve. Because of our sin, we deserve immediate death and hell. I think of the game Monopoly when someone draws the dreaded card from the community chest or chance pile. You know which one I'm talking about. It says, *"Go directly to jail. Do not pass go. Do not collect two hundred dollars."* There is an immediate consequence for pulling this card. In life, if we got what we truly deserve, then we would not be given another breath. We would have to face the immediate consequences of our sin. *But God!* Ephesians 2 says, *"But God, being rich in mercy, because of the great love with which he loved us, even when we were dead in our trespasses, made us alive together with Christ—by grace you have been saved."*[46] He gives us mercy and grace that we do not deserve.

God intervenes by sending Jesus. Mark 10:45 says, *"For even the Son of Man came not to be served but to serve, and to give his life as a ransom for many."*[47] In the same way, we should give our lives to serve God and the people around us. Jesus served all––even his betrayer, Judas. Jesus went through some real turmoil in his serving, a lot more than carrying 150 gallons of water. I know that you are not Jesus, but you do have the Spirit of God within you if you are a believer and follower of Jesus. He helps us in our weakness, and we are often weak in our serving. Let us ask God to give us the servant's heart of Jesus, so that we might experience the fullness of God in our life of service. Pray for love, willingness, and opportunities to serve. And when God speaks, *"do whatever he tells you."*

1. Where in your life could you be serving the world around you?
2. What is holding you back from serving? (Time, willingness, laziness, lack of care, etc.)
3. Who is one person in your life that you could go out of your way to serve?

CHAPTER 5

Martha, Martha

Have you ever been to New York City, or even Las Vegas? These cities are pretty gnarly. The word that I think of when these cities come to mind is the word *hustle*. These cities go hard with everything that they do. It's like they never stop. Seriously, you can be in the city at 3 a.m. and there will be something happening. Las Vegas is known as "the entertainment capital of the world." This means it will grab your attention and keep it as long as it can. It could be the shows, casinos, or even the resorts. No matter what it is, the industry will fight for you to be satisfied with your time in their city. New York City has many nicknames, but my favorite is *"The city that never sleeps."* This nickname embodies the essence of the city's hustle mentality. It is filled with people who are hustling to make their dreams come true. Companies who want to win your love, loyalty, and of course, your money. The more you hustle, the more approval you receive from the world around you. Unfortunately, this is a vicious cycle that continues over and over again.

I currently work for an amazing organization called Ride Nature.[48] I could not be more proud to work for such a Christ-centered, God-glorifying ministry. We use action sports like surfing, skateboarding, wakeboarding, and snowboarding, to reach people with the gospel of Jesus all over the world. It's incredible.

The other day I had the thought that Ride Nature is like New York. It's the ministry that never sleeps. I am no exception to this; I like to be busy. Let me just briefly inform you on some of the normal areas of ministry that we have going on at Ride Nature, just to give you a glimpse into the busyness. We host a Bible Study that we call *Skate Church* at five different skate parks around Southwest Florida every week, Monday through Friday. Some of those skate parks are an hour away from our headquarters. We have a Bible Study that we call *Wake Church* at the local wakeboard park every other week. We also host a *Surf Church* Bible Study twice a month all the way on the other coast of Florida about three hours one way, as well as a mountain bike ministry on Wednesdays that we call *Dirt Church*. Then, we host two separate men and women Bible Studies called *Men's Upper Room* and *Shred Sisters* on Mondays and Tuesdays, and a weekly homeless outreach on Thursday mornings that we call the *Homies Bible Study*. Plus, random outreach events like skateboard contests, worship nights, and community outreach. Did I mention that we have a full-service surf, skate, coffee, and retail shop with a skate park outside called *The House of Ride Nature?*[49] I almost forgot about our private indoor skate park--*The Ends*--where we give free access to the public. Oh, and we have a six-month discipleship program for 18-24 year olds wanting to grow in their walk with Jesus while learning how to use their love for action sports as a tool for ministry. These discipleship students stay at our headquarters for six months while attending classes and teachings to grow in their faith and leadership in ministry. We even hosted a conference this year called *A Call To Action Conference* where we gathered ministry leaders from all over the world to train, equip, and encourage them in ministry.[50] Ugh, I almost forgot to share that we also lead over 20 mission trips a year to places all over the world, partnering with other action sports ministries in order to train, reach, inspire, pioneer, and serve them.

    I am sure that this is just a hint of the things that we do at Ride Nature, but it's probably pretty clear to you that we are busy. Being in any ministry is generally pretty busy. People say that a ministry role is a 24/7, 365 job. But is this biblical? Well, yes and no.

    Yes, we are always working for the Lord, constantly dying to ourselves in order to serve Christ. We are also serving to the best of our ability. Colossians 3:23 says, *"Whatever you do, work heartily, as for the Lord and not for men."*[51] This is how we are to serve in ministry. We are to give our best; we are to hustle. Why would we not hustle when the Lord has called us to such a great ministry of reconciliation? We hustle for the Lord.

    But also, no. 24/7 is the call for our dedication to Christ, but not necessarily to our ministry role. I want to be clear that I am a huge advocate for hard work and dedication to the ministry role that you serve in. But Jesus shows us that there is a time for rest and a time for spending it with him. I want to go through these two very important areas of life as we follow Jesus out of my love for you and your personal walk with Christ.

Let's first talk about rest. As I write this book, I am currently on sabbatical. This is the 7th year that I have been in my ministry role, and our organization has graciously given me a much-appreciated sabbatical for three months. In fact, it has been very restful and even therapeutic in a way to write this book. The word *sabbatical* actually comes from the biblical term *Sabbath*, which is a day of rest in the week for the Judeo-Christian people. We receive the Sabbath from the Law of Moses and of course, the Ten Commandments. The 4th commandment is to remember the Sabbath day and keep it holy. God only gave Ten Commandments for the Israelites to live by, and he saw it fit that out of all the commands he could give, remembering the Sabbath and keeping it holy would make the top ten. This must mean that it is important to God, and important for us.

God himself gave us an example of this in the creation narrative in the book of Genesis. God created the heavens and the earth and everything in it for six days, and on the seventh day he rested. Not that God needed a day to rest, but he was giving us an example of what our lives should look like. In fact, Jesus is quoted in the gospel of Mark as saying, *"The Sabbath was made for man, not man for the Sabbath."*[52] This shows that God gives us this commandment for our benefit. This is not a chore or something that should be burdensome. It is a day of rest gifted to us by our loving God for our good.

Let's be real, how many people actually set aside a day to rest every week? Out of all of the Christians you know, how many of them really have a Sabbath day of rest? I am not talking about a day to go to church. I am talking about a day of real rest. There's always something going on. Life is busy. We can't stop doing things. Or, we are afraid that we are going to miss out on something or fall behind because we chose to take a break and rest.

When I ask people how they are doing, I usually get one of two common answers. The first is some form of "I've been good." The second is "I've been busy." It seems that everyone has a busy life, because that's the way America works. When people think about rest or Sabbath, they think the wrong way. Most people think that rest is equivalent to laziness. This is just not true. Look at Chick-fil-A. They ranked 3rd in revenue for fast food in 2022 only behind McDonalds and Starbucks.[53] Get this––they achieved this *while* having a company-wide Sabbath. Closed on Sundays. Every time I pass a Chick-fil-A, they are busy. The only time they are not busy is when they are closed. Sometimes, we also need to be "closed."

It should be a priority for us to take a weekly day of Sabbath. Pick a day––*any* day––and make it your day of rest. Make it a day that you only do things that are restful; nothing burdensome, and nothing draining. Think of a pit stop in a Formula 1 race. These drivers are incredibly talented and they are focused on their objective to be the first to cross the finish line; but every single one of them stops during the race. Stopping during a race seems odd, but here's the fact: if you don't stop, you can't win. You will inevitably either run out of fuel or burn out your tires. Maybe even both! If either of these things happen, your race is over. The fuel can be predictable; there are gauges that will tell you when the fuel is low. But the tires can only be felt by the driver or seen by others. The pit stop for the tires could be different from race to race depending on the track, season, weather, or even who is driving.

In the same way, we need to take pit stops in our lives. We need to refuel on a regular basis so we can continue moving forward. Take a Sabbath day that allows you to refuel, and while you refuel, assess any other adjustments that you need to make. Maybe the tires on your Funmobile need to be changed. Maybe your social wagon needs a new spoke, or your introverted motorcycle needs a new wheel. Whatever it is, pause and make the change so you can continue on your race. These things can all bring you rest, which is a gift from God. Find what rest you need and make it happen.

Sometimes whatever is restful for you—whether it's abstaining from tiresome tasks, refueling your social meter, or reading that book you have been looking forward to—can be restful in itself, but even in these things alone you'd be missing a major component of rest. Jesus says in Matthew 11:28, *"Come to me, all who labor and are heavy laden, and I will give you rest."*[54] If you want some real rest, you can only find it in Jesus himself. Sure, if you kick back on the couch and watch Netflix all day for Sabbath, you might feel *some* sense of rest. But Jesus says that we will find rest for our souls if we come to him. That's the kind of rest that we are looking for. Rest that lasts longer than one Sunday afternoon.

Psalm 23 gives us a beautiful picture of what resting in the Lord looks like. It starts by saying *"The Lord is my shepherd; I shall not want"*[55] Some other versions say, *"The Lord is my shepherd; I lack nothing."* Do we truly believe when we are with Jesus and have him as our shepherd, we lack nothing? We might believe this at heart, but often we act like we are still missing something. We act like we need Jesus…and X, Y, and Z. The truth is that if and when we have Jesus, we lack nothing. This is actually the opposite of what we normally think. When we look for rest in other things outside of Jesus, we still have this longing because we are only getting minor glimpses of rest. We are then seeking the gift over the Giver.

This is what Psalm 23 says next: *"He makes me lie down in green pastures. He leads me beside still waters. He restores my soul."*[56] I love the symbolism of God doing all of the work here. We are portrayed as sheep, and it is the shepherd that gives the rest. First, the shepherd *makes* us lie down. This gives the picture of us not wanting to rest, or the feeling that we don't really need to. But God knows what we need, and he makes us rest.

I think of nap time for my son, Zephyr. Often, when his naptime is approaching, he doesn't think he needs to nap, nor does he want to take a nap. Does this mean that he should skip his nap? Absolutely not. In fact, if he skips his nap, I know that the rest of the day will be a complete disaster. So what happens in this situation? I make him nap. I know what is best for him in this situation; as his father, I know what he needs. How much more does the Lord, our Good Shepherd, know what we need?

Next, the Psalm says he *leads* us. So, first the Lord makes us rest, and then when we have received our much needed rest, he leads us to be refreshed. It's like when my son wakes up from a nap, the first thing that he asks for is cold water. He loves to have a refreshing drink of water after he has woken up from his restful sleep. So, I lead him to the kitchen to get a cup of cold water. This is the picture that we get from this passage.

Lastly, it says that he *restores my soul.* Again, I love that it is God doing all of the work. God is the one that brings soul restoration. Without God doing these things, we would not be able to have our soul restored. The harsh reality is that sin wreaks havoc in our lives, but especially in our souls. Sometimes when we sin, there may be no external effects in our lives. Maybe no one else was damaged in your sin—but you were. There is no amount of sleep that could restore the damages of sin in your soul. Physical rest does not equal restoration of the soul, only Jesus can do that.

Maybe you feel ashamed to seek rest in the Lord because you know that in your sin, you have grieved God. Well, there is good news for us! God *wants* us to come to him to find restoration from our sin. You see, God loves us and wants us to draw near to him. God is not afraid of our sin. He came to earth to confront sin and defeat it once and for all. He conquered sin for you and me. If we think that anything else can restore our souls from the sin that has damaged it, we would be so wrong.

Let's look at another passage in the Bible that I think of most when it comes to the difference between resting and hustling. It's the story of Mary and Martha. The story of these two followers of Jesus is so convicting to me. Mainly because I know that I am a Martha type of person, and I need to be a Mary.

This story is found in Luke chapter 10 where Jesus has been invited into the house of a woman named Martha. As Jesus begins to teach Martha's guests, Martha's sister Mary decides to sit at Jesus' feet and listen to his teaching with them. Verse 40 says that Martha was *"distracted with serving."*[57]

This passage is so interesting because we almost always see serving in scripture as the best option for us. But in this situation, it says that Martha is *distracted* with serving. Maybe she was cleaning up or getting her guests something to eat or drink. We really aren't informed on how she is serving, but what we do know is that it was distracting her from spending time with Jesus. While hustling, Martha gets frustrated that her sister is not helping her serve. Martha thinks that her sister Mary is *distracted* from serving, but it was actually Martha that was distracted from Jesus.

At this point Martha is not only feeling frustrated, but also self-righteousness. Martha is so sure that she is correct in her assessment of the situation that she approaches Jesus while he is teaching and gives him quite a talking to. Martha says to Jesus, *"Lord, do you not care that my sister has left me to serve alone? Tell her then to help me."*[58] Yikes.

We can start with the accusation that Martha throws at Jesus. She is accusing him of not caring for her or her sister. Well, this is certainly not the truth. We actually see in John 11:5 that *"...Jesus loved Martha and her sister and Lazarus."*[59] So we can be sure that Jesus loved them. But isn't this what we often do when things aren't going the way we want them to? We place blame on others and sometimes even God, especially when we are doing things that we believe are good and righteous, like serving. We feel like we should be repaid for our good works.

It's a bold move to accuse Jesus, but it might be even more bold to try to command him to do something, which is what Martha did next. She gives Jesus a command: *"Tell her then to help me."*[60] This is coming from Martha's assumption that she is correct in her belief that her sister is in the wrong and that she is in the right. By assuming this, Martha is fully expecting this command to be met by Jesus' mutual agreement and even a submission to her request. As for all of the others who are there listening to Jesus, they probably are expecting the same as Martha—but Jesus was different.

Jesus sees the whole picture. Not only does he see the actions of one person, but he also sees the intentions of their heart. Jesus weighs the intentions of the heart between Mary and Martha. We can tell by Jesus' response that Martha has a lot going on. Jesus says, *"Martha, Martha, you are anxious and troubled about many things, but one thing is necessary. Mary has chosen the good portion, which will not be taken away from her."*[61]

Jesus knows that Martha is anxious and troubled about many things. He sees that she has a skewed perspective and understanding of the situation. Martha is serving out of obligation, with a short temper and an anxious heart. Again, let's remember that she is distracted with serving—even serving Jesus himself.

Jesus is so sweet in his response to Martha. He meets her in her troubles and chaos and says, *I see you.* But Jesus doesn't simply acknowledge her hurt and leave her there; he calls her to a better place. Jesus reminds Martha of the truth that only *one* thing is necessary. He reminds her that the good portion is found sitting at the feet of Jesus. You have nothing to bring, no acts of service, no gifts or talents. You need only to sit and receive from Jesus. Charles Spurgeon once shared a sermon and told his congregation, *"You are very diligent in your religion, you are attentive to all its outward rites and ceremonies, you believe the articles of your church, you practice the ceremonies ordained by its rulers; but, but, do you know that all this is nothing, unless you sit at Jesus' feet?"*[62]

This is a caring pastor who is first and foremost looking for the spiritual well-being of his congregation. A lot of pastors look for the well-being of their ministry outreach before the well-being of the congregation, and this is why there is a lot of burnout in ministry. If not burnout, then you get a lot of Marthas. Jesus calls us to serve only after we have sat at his feet and have learned from him, been restored by him, and have received love from him.

You can have a church or a ministry full of Marthas, and the thing is, it will probably look great. But you don't want that, trust me. You want a church or ministry full of Marys. What we need to understand is that there is truly only *one* thing that is necessary, and that one thing is sitting at the feet of Jesus. To know him and be known by him. To be a lover, follower, seeker, learner, and friend of Jesus: this is the one and only necessary thing. All other things are extracurricular at best, and at worst could be sinful. We need to remember that Jesus doesn't need us for anything. Isaiah 64:6 says, *"All our righteous deeds are like a polluted garment."*[63] This gives us a word picture of our "righteous deeds" being as good as a dirty diaper.

I'm not saying that we should all just stop serving. I am simply echoing Jesus in saying there is only one thing that is necessary. It is only after you have sat at the feet of Jesus that you are able to serve in a healthy way. I know I have felt a lot like Martha at times. I feel as though I am working so hard in my serving and I get frustrated when I don't see others doing the same. I find myself having a short temper and confronting God about my struggles. God always meets me in the same way that he met Martha, saying, *"Brooks, Brooks you are anxious and troubled about many things, but one thing is necessary."* To this response, I agree with the Father and take a seat at his feet where I can get the necessary Bread of Life that I need.

We can clearly see here that Jesus views rest and service differently. These two areas of life are both a calling and command from the Lord. I believe that Jesus was a hard worker, but he knew when to take his time to rest. He was the definition of intentional. He cared more about ministry than we could ever imagine, yet he was never in a hurry unless it was to be alone with God. Jesus commands us to rest, but to rest in him. Jesus calls us to slow down and focus on what really matters in the situation. We see Jesus oftentimes withdrawing from everyone around him, including ministry opportunities, to go be with the Lord in prayer. He gave us this example to show that we, too, should take time to be with the Lord and let him revive our souls. We can know that if Jesus did this, we should also follow in this and sit at the Lord's feet. To take it a step further, we should encourage this in others as well. Let's not judge or look down on those who are taking time out of serving to be with Jesus. I am not encouraging laziness. I am promoting intentional time with Jesus over ministry. So take a Sabbath, set aside the first hour of the morning, refocus yourself on Jesus, let him revive your soul. After, and only after you have done this, can you serve with the heart of Christ. If we can make this change, we will look different. Not because you are skimping out of ministry, but because your ministry will produce more fruit. You will only be more effective in your ministry if you are effective with your personal time with Jesus.

1. Have you sat at Jesus' feet lately?
2. Do you identify more with Martha or Mary in this season of life?
3. What can you do this week to make a move from being like Martha to being like Mary?

CHAPTER 6

Burn and Scuttle the Boats

Jesus was a radical. He also called his followers to a radical life. In today's world, being known as a "religious radical" is typically frowned upon, feared, and even discouraged. I am a guy who likes radical things and radical people. Radical people remind me of action sports junkies like myself. They tend to live life to the extreme and while others look at them and think they are absurd, they also admire them. Let's remember that Jesus was so different that he was resented and reviled. But the radical way of life that Jesus calls people to is not the radical life that other religions call for. Is it extreme? Absolutely. Is it hard? No doubt. Is it different? Definitely.

I absolutely love Steve Jobs' quote about these kinds of people. *"Here's to the crazy ones. The misfits. The rebels. The troublemakers. The round pegs in the square holes.*

The ones who see things differently. They're not fond of rules. And they have no respect for the status quo. You can quote them, disagree with them, glorify or vilify them. About the only thing you can't do is ignore them. Because they change things. They push the human race forward. And while some may see them as the crazy ones, we see genius. Because the people who are crazy enough to think they can change the world, are the ones who do."[64]

Now this is a quote that makes me feel like getting more extreme in my walk with Jesus. Do you resonate with this quote at all? Maybe you thought of someone specific when you read this quote. Maybe you see yourself as one of these people. If not, that's okay. I see myself as one of these kinds of people, in a way. I have not always been fond of rules. I, at times, have felt like a misfit and often act as a rebel. Maybe it's just the way that God made me, but this is who I am, and these are my people.

I played many different team sports in high school, but my main sport growing up was wakeboarding. One weekend, I had a big wakeboard contest at the same time as a soccer tournament. I wasn't the best player on our soccer team, but I was the highest scorer on the team—probably because I wasn't afraid to shoot and I was a bit of a ball hog. Anyway, I had a choice to make. I could let the whole team down and go to the wakeboard contest, or be a team player but live with the regret of not following my heart by going to my wakeboard contest. Let's just say that my team wasn't very happy with me, but my heart was full. I went against the grain, and to my teammates, I was one of the wild ones—a rebel—but I could not be ignored. My presence or my absence was felt.

I think of Jesus when I hear this Steve Jobs quote. He was so different, and he was radical in how he did things. *"You can quote them, disagree with them, glorify or vilify them. About the only thing you can't do is ignore them."* This is so true about Jesus! Jesus was that much of a standout that no one could ignore him. Even to this day, two thousand years later, you would be hard pressed to find anyone who has heard of Christianity not having an opinion on Jesus, be it good, bad, or indifferent. I see in scripture that Jesus is constantly calling his followers to live in this different way. Jesus calls us to not live the status quo, but to live radically different for him.

Have you ever heard of a man named Ernest Shackleton? He was one of the greatest explorers and pioneers of all time. He was Irish born but lived in England. This man was full of wonder and he had the courage to fulfill his wonderful dreams. He had this radical dream of pioneering the South Pole of Antarctica. Now, this was something that not a single soul had ever accomplished. He, of course, could not tackle this journey alone; he was going to need a crew of sailors, scientists, and fellow explorers. So, Ernest decided to post an ad in the London Times newspaper to recruit his crew. This is what the ad said: *"Men wanted for hazardous journey. Low wages, bitter cold, long hours of complete darkness, constant danger, safe return doubtful, honour and recognition in case of success."*[65]

What do you think? Would you respond well to this advertisement? He is calling radical people like himself. He wanted to weed out all of the softies that just wanted the glory for the exploration without the difficulty. He knew that the thought of an adventurous exploration would sound great to most people, but he wanted to let them know the reality of the situation from the beginning. This is going to be dangerous, so dangerous that I doubt that we will even make it back safely. It will not be easy. Are you willing to suffer physically, mentally, and financially? Because if you come on this trip with me, you will suffer in all of these ways. But there is some great news: if you are willing to accept this offer and go on the journey of a lifetime, you will receive honor and recognition for being one of the pioneers of the South Pole!

Do you think that he got any responses from this advertisement? Well, supposedly he was flooded with over 5,000 responses! Men from all over were chaotic enough to accept such a radical offer. People willing to take a chance on reaching the icy southern tip of the world.

You want to hear something even cooler? They made it! Ernest Shackleton and his crew founded the South Pole in Antarctica. I am certain that many of you have never heard the name Ernest Shackelton before, and I would bet that none of you could name the rest of his crew members. All of this to say, they changed the world but their glory was short lived. They have since long been forgotten.

Believe it or not, Jesus calls his followers to a similar journey in life. This is something that is not typically the topic of discussion in most churches or discipleship courses, but it's very important to go over this stuff. I am going to be real with you. Much like Ernest Shackleton, if Jesus had a wanted ad, it would frighten most readers. I just want to share some verses and look at the harsh truth of what we are called to as Christ followers.

2 Timothy 3:12 says, *"Indeed, all who desire to live godly in Christ Jesus will be persecuted."*[66] Let's just start here. You will be persecuted. Sounds fun, right? You want to live a godly life following Jesus? Well, then you need to be aware and ready to be persecuted by the world around you. The great missionary Hudson Taylor once said, *"Carrying the cross does mean following in Jesus' footsteps. And in His footsteps are rejection, broken heartedness, persecution and death. There are not two Christs - an easy going one for easy going Christians, and a suffering one for exceptional*

believers. There is only one Christ. Are we willing to follow His lead?"[67]

Luke 14:33 is another sobering verse: *"So then, none of you can be my disciple who does not give up all his own possessions."*[68] Okay, so be ready to forfeit your possessions. This isn't exactly literal, but it is a call to give up anything that God asks you to give up. Christ will provide your every need, so don't trust the possessions, but trust your Provider. If God calls you to give up something, even something that you highly value, then you must trust him and give it up. Have open hands to let go of or receive whatever Jesus wills. I promise you he is worth far more than all of your possessions combined.

Then there's Matthew 10:38. *"And he who does not take his cross and follow after me is not worthy of me."*[69] This is a heavy one. Jesus is literally saying here, *be willing to die on my behalf.* Pick up your shameful and torturous killing device and follow in my footsteps as I lead you into an evil world that will gladly take the cross that you carry and nail you to it. Again, this verse seems unsettling; but only if you don't truly believe that Jesus is leading you to a place of eternal life, even if it is through a viscous, worldly death. Leonard Ravenhill once said in a sermon, *"We have never seen the agonizing death of a man on a cross. Immediately a man was nailed to a cross, he lost all his rights. And if you ever get nailed to a cross, you'll lose all yours too."*[70] Ravenhill was talking about the moment that you figuratively died to yourself. You decided to literally change your way of life to agree daily with Jesus' prayer in the garden before going to the cross of saying, *"Nevertheless, not my will, but yours, be done."*[71]

The most alarming thing is that this verse, in most people's eyes, is not the worst of the lot. The worst of all for most people is found a few verses earlier in Matthew

10:22 which says, *"You will be hated by everyone because of me."*[72] If there is one thing that people don't want, it is to be hated by others. We all want to be loved. Not only do we want to be loved, but we want to be admired. Jesus knows this about us which is why he forewarns us. He knows that we crave the praise of man. Jesus is being straightforward with us: when we truly follow him in his teachings, commands, and truths, we will in return be hated by others.

We could go on and on, but I think that these verses should be enough to chew on for a bit. So, if we took these verses and compiled them to create an advertisement to follow Jesus, it would sound something like this: *"Men wanted to follow Jesus. Persecution guaranteed. Must give up everything, elevating Jesus himself as the only real value to your life. On your journey you will need to be prepared to die on behalf of Jesus. And because of this, you will be hated by all who oppose your choice to follow Jesus."*

Sounds fun, right? But wait, there's more! No, not more verses about hardships, although we could definitely list more of those. These are more uplifting and hopeful verses. There are some major pieces to the puzzle that we're currently missing that won't just balance the scale, but tip it completely.

John 11:25-26 says, *"Jesus said to her, "I am the resurrection and the life; he who believes in me will live even if he dies, and everyone who lives and believes in me will never die. Do you believe this?"*[73] What a great question to ask after Jesus makes this promise. He promises eternal life to all who will accept this call and then he asks, *do you believe this?* You would have to in order to accept the call to follow Jesus, right? If you do believe, you will have eternal life––as in you live forever. This alone outweighs all of the verses that we have listed thus far. Who cares if I need to be prepared to die? I have eternal life with Jesus, even if I do!

How about this one? Matthew 19:29 says, *"And everyone who has left houses or brothers or sisters or father or mother or children or lands, for my name's sake, will receive a hundredfold and will inherit eternal life."*[74] Jesus is saying that if you choose to follow him, you will receive a hundredfold of anything that you forfeited to follow Jesus. I know nothing about investments in stocks or crypto currency, but this sounds like an investor's dream. So, if you think that you are missing out or losing in life by following Jesus, think again. The Lord promises that following him will be for your benefit at the end of the day. And then, he again doubles down on the eternal life portion of the deal.

We could list so many verses that speak to the promises of all of the many benefits of life with Jesus, such as peace, love, hope, joy, and more. But I want to end the ad with a familiar wording from Ernest's advertisement. In Matthew 10:32, Jesus says, *"Whoever acknowledges me before others, I will also acknowledge before my Father in heaven."*[75] In other words, honor and recognition. Your name, written in the book of life forever. When your earthly life has ended and you come face to face with God, Jesus will acknowledge you before the Father. Jesus will claim you in front of the Father and he will say, *"Well done my good and faithful servant."*[76]

Now, let's take one last look at what this advertisement for Jesus might look like, but this time with these verses added. *"Men wanted to follow Jesus. Persecution guaranteed. Must give up everything, elevating Jesus himself as the only real value to your life. On your journey you will need to be prepared to die on behalf of Jesus. And because of this, you will be hated by all who oppose your choice to follow Jesus. You will receive a hundredfold back of anything that you gave up to follow Jesus. Eternal life starts the moment that you accept this call by putting your faith in Jesus. Honor and recognition will be given to you before the only true God who loves you and created you for this journey."*

I like to make pros and cons lists in order to weigh a lot of decisions, like which grill to purchase or where to go on vacation, but this one is a no-brainer. The pros far outweigh the cons when it comes to following Jesus. And even the things that we see as cons are actually not cons at all; they are actually good for us. Things like persecution and suffering make us more like Jesus. Giving up our possessions only makes us more dependent on God, and that is a very good thing. The problem today is that we never inform new believers about the journey that they are signing up for; we only tell them about the destination. It is important to share the whole truth about following Jesus. John was the only apostle who was not martyred for his life of following Jesus, but he was still exiled to an island to live alone. Living a life following Jesus will not be easy, but it will be worth it. But don't take it from me––John and the other apostles who suffered for Jesus' names sake would tell you the same thing.

I want to share one more story with you about an explorer named Hernan Cortés. He was a Spanish conquistador who explored the Americas, but is most known for his founding and conquering of the city of Veracruz, Mexico. He brought all of his shipmates on to land to settle and eventually conquer the Aztec people. Once he had all of the people safely on shore, he ordered some of the men to go back to the boats to burn and scuttle (sink) the ships.[77] This was probably a big surprise to his crew as they watched their ships burning and sinking right before their very eyes while they were on shore. Cortés did this for a reason; he was making a definitive statement. He was saying, *We are here to stay. We won't leave. We can't leave. There's no turning back.* Talk about a bold move from Cortés. He meant business; he was there to conquer and pioneer the land. Any escape route or plan B would only give opportunity to retreat, and he wasn't going to let that even be an option. He let go of all that was behind him and he wasn't looking back.

Similarly, the prophet Elisha was called to serve God––no turning back. Elisha was a rich man who had a great life. How do I know that he was rich? Well, the story in 1 Kings Chapter 19 says that he has 12 pairs of oxen.[78] 24 oxen would be worth a lot in today's day and age, how much more must it have been worth in the biblical times? Even with his earthly success, God called him to a life that was even better. The prophet Elijah comes along and calls Elisha to follow after him in order to become a prophet of the Lord. Elisha had a tough choice to make. He could stay in his comfortable life of material wealth, or he could sacrifice all that he had and follow God's call for his life and trust that God had a better plan.

So what did he do? He slaughtered the oxen, burned the plow, and cooked the meat. He got rid of his old life. Total surrender to God's call. You could probably guess that this paid off for him. Big time. Do you have any idea who has the most recorded miracles out of all the prophets in the Old Testament? That would be Elisha. Right before his teacher Elijah was miraculously taken up to heaven by God, he asked Elisha what he could do for him before he left. So Elisha asked, *"Please let there be a double portion of your spirit on me."*[79] Elijah left this earth having eight recorded miracles. Want to guess how many miracles Elisha had? You guessed it: 16. You want to

Burn and Scuttle the Boats

hear something even weird? Elisha died when he was one miracle short of his *"double portion."* But 2 Kings 13:21 tells us the rest of the story, *"And as a [dead] man was being buried, behold, a marauding band was seen and the [dead] man was thrown into the grave of Elisha, and as soon as the [dead] man touched the bones of Elisha, he revived and stood on his feet."*[80] Elisha got his double portion, but it wasn't until after he had died. God is faithful and we can trust him with our lives.

So, what about you and your life? Are you holding onto things from your past? Do you have any habits left over from your old life of sin and death? Do you have any fear of fully stepping into this life with Jesus? The Israelites were promised by God that they could go to the Promised Land; a land that was flowing with milk and honey. They received this promise that they would take the land and be successful, but they were afraid. They had fear because the land was inhabited by giants and they knew that it would be a battle. The Israelites were all mixed up in their thinking. Instead of yearning for freedom in the Promised Land, they began to look backwards and wished that they could go back to slavery where they had garlic and onions. I love garlic and onions, but if I were a slave, I'd trade them for my freedom any day. They lost sight of the fact that God had already promised them the victory and freedom. Are you believing in the promises of God, or are you looking at the obstacles in the way? Or maybe even past comforts that the Lord has asked you to leave behind?

Jesus doesn't want half of your life or half of your heart, he wants it all. He calls us to totally surrender to him and his will. So why would we only commit some parts to him? It simply comes down to our trust, or lack of trust, in Jesus and his promises. Here's the truth: Jesus says in John 16:33, *"In the world you will have tribulation.*

But take heart; I have overcome the world."[81] You will definitely have trials, tribulations, and troubles. Life with Jesus will not be easy, but it will be worth it. Our souls can be at ease because Jesus has already overcome the world. I know that living in this way is not a normal thing to do, but Jesus was different and he wants you to be different as well. Jesus doesn't want you to hold on to the past, he wants you to move forward with him. So, why hold on to any plan of retreat? Why not let go of the things that are tethering you to the old you before meeting Christ? Accept the call of the Lord on your life. Burn and scuttle the boats. Burn the plow and slaughter the oxen. The Lord will never let you down, and you will not regret it. I will leave you with the sweet and encouraging words of the apostle Paul found in 2 Corinthians 4:16-18: *"So we do not lose heart. Though our outer self is wasting away, our inner self is being renewed day by day. For this light momentary affliction is preparing for us an eternal weight of glory beyond all comparison, as we look not to the things that are seen but to the things that are unseen. For the things that are seen are transient, but the things that are unseen are eternal."*

1. Are you fully aware and accepting of what a life following Jesus entails?
2. What boats are still anchored in the port of your life?
3. What fears do you have in burning those boats?

CHAPTER 7

In Play at Little Games

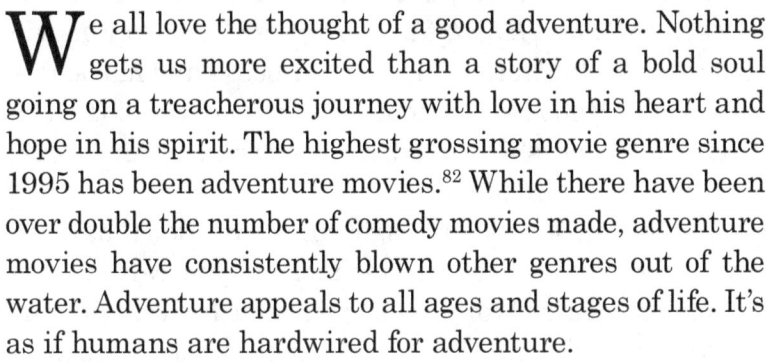

We all love the thought of a good adventure. Nothing gets us more excited than a story of a bold soul going on a treacherous journey with love in his heart and hope in his spirit. The highest grossing movie genre since 1995 has been adventure movies.[82] While there have been over double the number of comedy movies made, adventure movies have consistently blown other genres out of the water. Adventure appeals to all ages and stages of life. It's as if humans are hardwired for adventure.

Of course we all desire to be adventurous, but many of us are not. It's estimated that 70-80% of people in the world will never visit another country in their lifetime. For Americans, that number is closer to 40%.[83] We have so much access to international travel, yet almost half of the American population will never adventure to an unknown land.

I have had the privilege of traveling to over 30 countries. This has given me a broad sense of adventure. I have seen God's creation and his people all over the world. From the snow-capped Himalayan Mountains in Nepal, to the murky waters of the Nile River in Uganda, to the beautiful, barreling waves in El Salvador, I have seen God's creation around the globe. This is something that most people will never get to experience first-hand. I feel blessed to have gone on so many adventures in my lifetime, and I hope that others will have even greater ones themselves.

The fact is that while we all crave adventure, it mostly stays in our thoughts, imaginations, and dreams. We would love to be like Bilbo Baggins from J.R.R. Tolkien's *The Hobbit* who stepped out of his comfort zone and adventured into the unknown.[84] Bilbo crossed rivers and mountains, met all types of different people and creatures that he had only read about in books, faced dragons, overcame his fears, and even conquered his enemies. Here's a great quote from *The Hobbit: An Unexpected Journey* movie adaptation: "The world is not in your books and maps, it is out there."[85] Bilbo had the courage to take a step of faith by leaving his home shire and doing something adventurous, and he was rewarded for it.

We live in a day and age where we don't have to adventure. With all of our technology, you can see the 7 Wonders of the World from your couch through your phone. You don't have to leave your home for food, it can be brought to you with the movement of your thumb. You can even watch church without getting out of bed. It's easy to just chill and be comfortable, but Jesus doesn't call us to that. Jesus calls us to a deeper and more adventurous life.

I don't think that we are called to simply go on an adventure. While going on an adventure is fun and exciting, it can ultimately be meaningless. Like in Ecclesiastes when the teacher keeps repeating that it's all meaningless and chasing after the wind.[86] We are called to live meaningful lives for Jesus. Trust me when I say that living your life for him is a meaningful adventure. Actually, it's as meaningful as it can get. So, the difference isn't if you are adventurous or not, but if you are adventuring with Jesus or not.

It probably comes as no surprise to you that I love to read. Let me tell you, there are some pretty great books out there focused on devout Christ followers and their unimaginable lives living in obedience to Jesus. The best part about it is that these books are not made up fiction, they are true stories. This does not mean that these stories are always happy-go-lucky. In fact—spoiler alert—they are normally sad and full of suffering. But oddly enough, these stories oftentimes make us envious of their faith adventures with the Lord.

One of my favorite books is called *The Insanity of God* by Nik Ripken.[87] Nik Ripken is actually a nom de plume (a fake pen name) because some of these stories are so insane that he needed to protect his identity and the identities of others. When you read this book, and I hope that you do, you will be at the edge of your seat the whole time. He radically answers the call of Jesus to go where he calls, no matter what. His life is led by obedience to Jesus alone, and in his obedience, Jesus takes him on adventures that you would not even believe. Again, I must reiterate that this story, while incredible, it's not all sunshine and rainbows. His story is marked with suffering, persecution, sadness, and emotional poverty; but he has hope for a future rooted in a God who loves him and will never leave him.

Another book that I have really been inspired by is *The Hiding Place*.[88] This is an autobiography from

Corrie ten Boom, a Dutch Christian who helped hide Jewish people from the Nazi regime during the Holocaust in World War II. Her family went so far as to build a secret room in their home in order to conceal the Jewish people from the Nazi authorities. Again, this is not a happy story, but you can't argue that it is extremely inspiring. Corrie ended up getting caught and sent to a concentration camp. She went through some of the worst conditions imaginable, but she brought hope to those around her, because she had hope in Jesus. This is another book that I would recommend to everyone, but fair warning––you will probably feel like you should be doing a lot more for Jesus after reading it.

I have to mention one more story that I highly admire. Have you ever heard of the Free Burma Rangers? Their website states that "The Free Burma Rangers (FBR) is a multi-ethnic humanitarian service movement working to bring help, hope and love to people in the conflict zones of Burma, Iraq, and Sudan."[89] In my words, the FBR are fearless, humble, gnarly servants who run to danger in order to save others from it. These people are wild, in a good way. They are the kind of people that we look up to for their fearlessness. The founder and director's name is David Eubank. He was a ranger in the U.S. military and an officer in the Special Forces, but he grew up in a missionary family in Thailand. He ultimately decided to answer the call of Jesus to use the combination of his military expertise and love for God's people to help them both physically and spiritually.

One of the things I admire most is that the Eubanks do this as a family. David has led his wife and children on this adventure with Jesus. Just like his parents showed him how to reach the Thai people for Jesus during his upbringing, he now shows his children how to be obedient and fearless in following Jesus. There is a documentary film about their family and the Free Burma Rangers that documents the boldness of the FBR and their willingness to serve those being oppressed and bring them the hope of Jesus. I encourage you to give it a watch, and pray for them as they are constantly in dangerous warzones.

All of these stories are nothing short of incredible, and we all wish that we could live a life that is as bold as these. *So why don't we?* Don't get me wrong, I don't think that everyone can or even should be a David Eubank, but we can all be a servant of the Lord and see God move in and through our lives. The problem is that we all would rather watch, read, or hear about living a great and extraordinary life for Jesus than to actually experience it for ourselves. We are scared, and quite frankly, we are soft. Especially in the Western Church, we unfortunately have a lot of soft Christians. We think that the dangerous adventures with Jesus were only for the 12 apostles and today's missionaries.

So what does an adventure with Jesus look like for the average person who claims to be a Christian? Well, for starters, it looks a lot like church on Sunday and a prayer before meals. And if they are really adventurous, they might even join a small group. Sound familiar? Now, before we get too far, I want you to know that I am not trying to bash these people who faithfully attend church and pray before meals; I am actually stoked that they are doing so. But let's be honest, that is not very adventurous. I want them to experience more. I want *you* to experience more.

The Jesus Film did a research study asking 1,600 Christians what some of the hurdles are when it comes to sharing their faith.[90] The number one answer was fear. Do you want to know what the second highest answer was? *Nothing.* They said that there was nothing stopping them from sharing their faith, they just chose not to. If you want to start living a more adventurous life with Jesus, sharing your faith with people is an awesome start! This is a sure way to see God lead you to a new level of faith. Will it be easy? No. Will it be comfortable? Probably not. But it will be a blessing to you. This should be eye-opening to us as we look at how we can live a life that steps out in faith for Jesus.

Everyone loves games. Video games, board games, sports, cards, and every game in between, we can't get enough of them. Don't believe me? I'll put it into perspective for you. There are an estimated 285 million people who regularly watch esports (video games).[91] That many people watch other people play video games on a regular basis. In the year 2022, the gaming industry generated an estimated $184 billion while the music industry generated $26 billion and the movie industry generated $26 billion.[92] Gaming blew movies and music out of the water. I have one more quick stat for you, and this should really tell you how much we all love games. There are roughly eight billion people in the world. Five billion of those people engaged in watching a portion of the FIFA World Cup in 2022.[93] Now, these stats are only covering video games and soccer, and I am sure that many of you reading would not be a fan of either of those. I am also sure that you enjoy some other sport or playing another type of game.

I believe that we love games so much because it takes us away from everything else. It might be for a couple of hours, or even just a moment, but it removes ourselves from anything that we might deem "important." Our thoughts are temporarily put on hold in order to play or watch a game. We typically see this as a good thing, and we even use it as such. We come home after a long day of work, kick our feet up, and watch the game. Or, we feel like we need some social time, so we call up a few friends to host a game night. While this isn't inherently bad in and of itself, this can be a bad way of hiding from some very important things that God might be calling us to do. It could get in the way of our walk with Jesus.

There's a great poem by Robert D. Abrahams that he wrote in 1938 called "The Night They Burned Shanghai." [94] 1938 was the year before World War II began. Of course, World War II was the most destructive war in the history of the world. Abrahams writes a beautiful poem telling a story about a couple who are going across town to play cards with another couple. The man in the poem speaks of all of the places he would like to see around the world, like Athens, Naples, Copenhagen, Burma, Persia, Xanadu, Tivoli, Bucharest, and of course, Shanghai. But he keeps saying *"Tonight Shanghai is burning"* or *"Not Shanghai, they are burning that tonight."* He is basically saying, *I will never be able to see the Shanghai that I have heard so much about.* Why? Well, he has simply waited too long, and there are wars that are literally burning the city and killing its people. Abrahams is sad at the thought that he missed his chance to see Shanghai. It is pretty fascinating that he wrote this right before many of these cities burned and were unrecognizable after World War II, right? For me when I read this poem, I am not looking at it from the perspective of adventuring to new cities, but from the perspective of doing God's will in fulfilling the Great Commission. The last few stanzas in this poem are so powerful to me. I would like for us to take it in and really look at our own lives in light of these words:

Tonight they burn Shanghai, and we are safe –
Safe from the world and all its puzzles – safe
From everything except our own contempt.
Tonight Shanghai is burning,
And we are dying too.
What bomb more surely mortal
Than death inside of you?
For some men die by shrapnel,
And some go down in flames,
But most men perish inch by inch,
In play at little games.

Tonight, are you safe from the world and all its puzzles? I'm not talking about being safe from sin and death; if you are a believer in Jesus then you are indeed safe from sin and death. I am talking about safety from discomfort, persecution, and suffering for Jesus. Are you safe from having difficult conversations with your family or coworkers because you choose to avoid those conversations? Are you safe from being "canceled" because you have made the decision to keep quiet about your faith and the truths of scripture that might rub people the wrong way? Are you safe from everything except your own contempt (conscience), knowing that while you are safe, you are called to danger? Jesus tells us in Matthew 10, *"Behold, I am sending you out as sheep in the midst of wolves." (Matthew 10:16)*[95] This does not sound like safety to me. But Jesus continues to give us some great advice on how we are to enter into the danger: *"...so be wise as serpents and innocent as doves."* [96] Jesus is telling his disciples to be wise. Obviously there are wise and unwise times, places, and situations in which we should be sharing the gospel. Use wisdom. Pray, and then act. We are also called to be innocent. We should be as Jesus was when he was persecuted––blameless. If we are innocent and wise, we can mitigate the likelihood of danger. Notice that I said danger, not persecution. Also notice that I said mitigate, not eliminate. So, search your heart for any contempt inside of you, and pray that God will give you the will and ability to make a change.

"*Tonight Shanghai is burning, and we are dying too. What bomb more surely mortal than death inside of you?*"[97] Our earthly death is inevitable. We have a death bomb, and the timer has been set; yet we don't know when it will go off. The realization that time is of the essence must kick in for each of us. I have a tattoo of an hourglass on my right wrist as a constant reminder of this. There should be an urgency in fulfilling the Great Commission. James 4:14 tells us, "*...yet you do not know what tomorrow will bring. What is your life? For you are a mist that appears for a little time and then vanishes.*"[98] Our lives are equated to mist that is here one second and gone the next. Just like that, our life could be over and we're out of time. You cannot evangelize or make disciples in heaven––it must be done here and now. "*Tonight Shanghai is burning, and we are dying too.*"[99]

This last stanza is the most powerful of them all. "*For some men die by shrapnel, And some go down in flames, But most men perish inch by inch, In play at little games.*"[100] There are some people out there who die by doing unfathomably bold things for the Lord. If you are ready to read some remarkable stories of heroic faith, pick up a copy of *Foxe's Book of Martyrs*.[101] These are some of the most incredible stories of faithful believers who died for their faith in Jesus, some of which literally went down in flames. These are the few, or as Abrahams would say "some men," but this isn't the norm. The norm is what most men do. These men, Abrahams says, "*perish inch *by inch, In play at little games.*"[102] While he was playing cards, Shanghai was burning, and the rest of the world would be close behind it.

Let's look at this in a pure spiritual sense. The unbelieving world is about to burn. They are slaves to sin and death. There is no time to waste, for we do not know when their life will end; but when it does, they will enter into eternity. That eternity for an unbeliever will be a place of torment, punishment, weeping, and separation from God forever. They are getting closer and closer to that eternity every day that passes, and all the while they are playing little games, assuming that hell could never be in their future eternity.

For us who are believers, we need to look at our own lives and assess if we are using our time wisely. Are we playing little games while the world is burning? Much like the man in the poem who listed all of the places that he wanted to visit, we also should make a list of all of the unbelievers that we know and want to make into disciples of Jesus. Trust me when I say that the pain you *may* encounter for sharing your faith is far less than the pain you *will* feel if you do not, and that person passes into eternity without ever having the chance to respond to the gospel. This sadness will weigh much more heavily than even that man's in the poem who never saw Shanghai.

So what are the little games that you are playing? Maybe you golf three times a week for about four hours per round. You can do a lot with 12 hours per week. How many Netflix episodes do you watch every night? How much overtime do you put in at work trying to make enough money for that next big purchase? We all have little games that we play, and the first step is to name them.

For me, it's definitely my phone. My screen time far exceeds what I would like it to. If I used that time every day to engage in spiritual disciplines to grow spiritually or help others grow, I believe that my life would be blessed greatly. But instead, I play little games that are a distraction from what really matters in life. When we get to judgment day, I don't think that God is going to commend me for my ability to quote *The Office*.[103] In fact, I think that he will say that I could have and should have used that time so much more wisely. Ephesians 5:15-16 says, *"Look carefully then how you walk, not as unwise but as wise, making the best use of the time, because the days are evil."*[104] I think that the Lord would say that I was playing it safe by sitting in my home and watching TV while I could have gone on a grand adventure with Jesus. Are you in fear of going on a bold adventure with Jesus? Are you afraid of what he might ask you to do? Are you afraid of what other people might think of you?

Well, the will of God is the best place to be, so if God is calling you to do something or go somewhere, I would say to go for it. Let God show you his goodness through your obedience and faithfulness to his call. I'm about to ask you to do something, and I want you to be bold. Pray and ask God two things. First, ask the Lord what little games you are playing in your life that you need to lay down. You might not even need to pray this prayer; you might already know exactly what those little games are. Make a note of these and repent of them. Ask forgiveness for them, and receive the forgiveness that God will give you. To take it a step further, confess this to a friend and ask them to help hold you accountable.

Secondly—and this is the bold one—ask The Lord what his will is for your life. Ask God what your next step is in the adventure that he is calling you to. Maybe you have long been a believer but you have never followed the call to be baptized. This would be an amazing next step in your faith. Perhaps God is calling you to be more vocal about your faith with your family. If so, do it. Step into the unknown by sharing your faith. How wild would it be if God told you to pursue full-time missions? Maybe not just a mission trip, but moving to a different country to share the gospel with people across borders and across cultures. God might call you to change your career, serve at church, give your money or resources, sacrifice your comfort, or even to go join an organization like Free Burma Rangers. Boldly ask God to reveal his will for your life, *and then do it.*

I don't know what God will ask of you, but one thing that I do know is that you can trust him. Proverbs 3:5-6 says, *"Trust in the Lord with all your heart, and do not lean on your own understanding. In all your ways acknowledge him, and he will make straight your paths."*[105] God might ask us to do things that we don't understand, but we can trust him.

Jesus was different this way. He trusted God in all that he asked of him. He only did what the Father was doing. In John chapter 5 Jesus says, *"So Jesus said to them, "Truly, truly, I say to you, the Son can do nothing of his own accord, but only what he sees the Father doing. For whatever the Father does, that the Son does likewise. For the Father loves the Son and shows him all that he himself is doing."*[106] Jesus just wanted to do what the Father was doing, and we should want the same. Unfortunately, we all want to do what the rest of the world around us is doing. We want to be normal. We want to be safe. But Jesus wasn't normal or safe, he was different and daring. The Father called Jesus to live a life that showed life is not a game, it's a calling. You have a calling and God has planned a life for you that you could never even dream of. The question is, are you willing to do what God has planned for you, even though it will be different and daring? If he asks us to put down our little games, we can trust that he has something better for us. When God asks us to seek earthly discomfort, we can trust that God is going to provide spiritual comfort. If we acknowledge God's will, then he will lead us straight to the life that he wants for us. Please don't die––or let others die––by playing little games.

1. What are your little games?
2. What next step is God asking you to take in your walk with Jesus?

CHAPTER 8

The Prince of Peace Wielding a Sword

Peace is something that everyone searches and strives for. This is undoubtedly a good thing. I believe that when humanity is trying to bring peace, we are actually seeking the will of God. We love the thought of everyone having peace and living in peace with each other. There has been a running joke ever since the movie *Miss Congeniality* about world peace. The movie portrays a Miss USA beauty pageant where every contestant was asked the question, "What matters the most to you?" The joke is that every contestant in the pageant gave the same cliché answer: *world peace*. [107] It sounds great, and it is great; but it is not easy.

The Hebrew word for peace is *Shalom*. This is by far the

most well-known Hebrew word in the world, even by those who do not speak Hebrew. Shalom does mean peace, but this word is also used to say hello or goodbye. It is a way to tell someone that they are welcomed with peace, or that you hope that they have peace as they go about their day. It's a simple everyday word, but it actually has a deeper meaning. Saying shalom is not merely a greeting though, or a word that only means peace. Shalom oftentimes is translated as *well being* or *good health*. So, when a Jewish person says shalom, they are actually saying something more like, "May you have peace and well-being." Shalom can also mean *wholeness* or *completeness*. This gives us the idea that perfect peace is a life that is complete and whole.

The Bible is full of examples of what peace can look like. It even shows us how God blesses us with peace when we follow him. We can jump right into the scriptures to see the peace that we have access to. Isaiah 26:3 says, *"You keep him in perfect peace whose mind is stayed on you, because he trusts in you."*[108] God gives us perfect peace when we are fully looking to and trusting in him.

Perfect peace? Really? You mean, I have access to peace that is absolutely perfect? Yes! With all of the worry and anxiety that this life gives us, this passage is saying if we keep our thoughts and trust on God, he promises that he will keep us in perfect peace. That sounds amazing, but it's easier said than done. How often do we constantly have our minds set on Jesus? I don't know about you, but even when I stop to pray, my mind ends up thinking about other things within the first two minutes. It is not an easy task to keep our minds fully on Jesus at all times.

Psalm 34:14 tells us, *"Turn away from evil and do good; seek peace and pursue it."*[109] To seek out the wholeness that peace brings is something that seems to be found outside of evil. Even Jesus himself said that only God is good, so this tells us that God is peace and that only by seeking and pursuing him is where we will find real peace. Romans 8:6 reiterates this by saying, *"For to set the mind on the flesh is death, but to set the mind on the Spirit is life and peace."*[110] When we set our mind on the Spirit of God, we will have peace. It is the times that we are thinking about things that are not directly correlated with God and his goodness that we start to lack peace.

We all deal with troubles and hard times in life, both mentally and physically. But Philippians 4:6-7 tells us, *"Do not be anxious about anything, but in everything by prayer and supplication with thanksgiving let your requests be made known to God. And the peace of God, which surpasses all understanding, will guard your hearts and your minds in Christ Jesus."*[111] What an amazing thing, that we have direct access to peace at all times! God only asks that we bring those worries to him. When we bring these anxieties to the God of peace, he gives us the peace that only he can give, and that will guard our minds and hearts. Jesus himself tells us in John 14:27, *"Peace I leave with you; my peace I give to you. Not as the world gives do I give to you. Let not your hearts be troubled, neither let them be afraid."*[112] This peace is not the same peace that worldly things can give you. Peace that you might get from the world does not last. How much peace do you get from buying a new car? Sure, some peace of mind that your car probably won't break down for a while. But what about that new car payment you have? Do you still have peace when you need to pay that bill every month? What about 5-10 years down the road when your car starts having problems? Or, maybe you just want a change and you feel discontent. Is that car still giving you peace? Probably not. The peace from the world just doesn't last. How about a night out on the town after a long week just to let loose. Maybe you have some drinks, spend a little extra on dinner, and top it off with stopping for ice cream on the way home? Is that going to give you peace? And if so, for how long? Maybe until Monday when you have to go back to a job that you hate with people who you would refer to as co-workers instead of friends. I'm sorry, but that kind of peace is a cheap, bootleg, wish.com version of peace.

The peace that God gives is so good it's incomprehensible. Remember when Philippians says that this peace from God surpasses all understanding?[113] This means that we might be in the most dire circumstances, one where it seems that it would be impossible to have peace, but we can pray and bring those worries to God and ask him for peace and he will give it to us.

This peace is not merely for a moment or a season of life. This peace is eternal. The reason that we can have a peace that surpasses all understanding is because we know that this peace is one that will never leave us; it will go with us into eternity. Our peace is rooted in Jesus whom we have placed our faith and trust in, who has sealed our salvation through his death and resurrection. This is how we can have peace in the middle of trials and troubles, because we know that Jesus has sealed our eternity with him. Romans 5:1 says, *"Therefore, since we have been justified by faith, we have peace with God through our Lord Jesus Christ."*[114] Without Jesus, we cannot have real peace that lasts.

Now that we have observed the peace that we have as believers and followers of Jesus, let's talk about the peace that we are called to live out and bring to the world. We are called to have peace with others, even unbelievers. We will look at some verses to support and explain this. I want to say this up front: there is a fine line between living in peace and living in agreement. You can believe differently, disagree, and even be directly opposed to every choice that

Jesus Was Different

someone makes, yet it can still be possible for you to bring peace to them.

I know that this is hard for most people. I want to describe a few groups of thought that some of you might fall into, or even identify as. You might be someone who has decided to fully disengage from all people who believe differently than you. Whether you disagree with their religion, lifestyle, sexuality, politics, or any other part of their lives, you try your best to not associate with these people. You might even make fun of them and call them names. You probably like to gossip about these people to your friends, but you would never want to hang out with them. If that sounds like you, you are not alone; there are many people just like you. Maybe you are on the other end of the spectrum. Perhaps you would describe yourself as someone who thinks that everyone should not only coexist with all people and walks of life, but that we should also affirm them in their choices. I believe it's called the *Live Your Own Truth Movement*. Maybe you believe that truth is relative, and we should support and back the choices of others, regardless of our beliefs. If this sounds like you, again you are not alone. These two camps are typically very critical of the other, and for good reason, because both camps quickly find themselves in contempt with their own convictions.

A lot of you would probably say that you fall somewhere in the middle of these two camps. I expect that you resonate with one camp over the other, but you wouldn't agree with that camp fully. The truth is that neither of these camps are where you want to be. Jesus calls us to a different camp. I can't even really say that Jesus calls us to be somewhere in the middle, because Jesus is so very different in his approach. I want us to search the scriptures to see what God calls us to do, and also see Jesus' example.

Let's start with this insightful verse from Romans 12:18. *"If possible, so far as it depends on you, live peaceably with all."*[115] Some people might look at this verse and think that this is just a command to live at peace with other believers, but this verse is not talking only about believers. When it says to live peaceably with all, it means with all people everywhere in every walk of life, not just the body of believers. You might say, "Brooks, it's impossible to live peaceably with them! Well, the verse says "If possible, so far as it depends on you." This means that we are to give every effort to live peaceably with all people. You and I should never be the reason that there is no peace in a relationship, because it is our duty to do everything in our power––with Jesus––to live peaceably with all.

I feel like we are so often the ones who decide to withhold peace. If we're honest, we are the ones who make the decision to avoid people because we assume that there will be no peace in it. Because of this, we don't even try. This would be a failure when it comes to Romans 12:18. We are to make the effort to live peaceably with all, regardless of how the other person may or may not react. I love that this verse also says "if possible," as if to say that living peaceably is not always attainable. Peace is not up to one person, it must be two sided. The other person might not want to live peaceably, but that is their prerogative. We can only control ourselves, and I believe this verse is saying just that. It should be our goal to live peaceably with all.

In the Sermon on the Mount, Jesus gives the beatitudes and all of them are somewhat counter-cultural to what the listeners were used to hearing. Jesus says, *"Blessed are the peacemakers, for they shall be called sons of God."*[116] I see a lot of Christians who would be more known as peace *breakers* than peace*makers*, and that's unfortunate.

Making peace is not about agreeing to other beliefs or actions; it is about bringing peace in spite of disagreeing.

Jesus was ridiculed for this by the scribes, Pharisees, and other religious people. He lived out this teaching of living peaceably with all people, and others didn't like it. The religious leaders were recorded in Mark 2 questioning Jesus' way of bringing peace, saying, *"Why does he eat with tax collectors and sinners?"*[117] This baffled the religious leaders. They had already heard of Jesus speaking truth with authority and they saw him perform miracles, yet they did not understand why he would spend time with people who were so opposed to the truth––or rather, *their* truth. Jesus then brings a simple but profound analogy that explains the reason for his actions. In verse 17 Jesus responds, *"And when Jesus heard it, he said to them, "Those who are well have no need of a physician, but those who are sick. I came not to call the righteous, but sinners."* [118]

Jesus gives them a new perspective. He sees sinners as people who are helpless and hopeless. He saw the people around him differently than the Pharisees did; he saw them through the lens of love. If you want to live peaceably with sinful people, you have to be willing to engage with sinful people. Since when does scoffing at people bring them closer? Or when has rolling your eyes after hearing someone's beliefs ever brought about peace? Again, you don't have to, nor should you, agree or affirm their opposing beliefs, but you should live peaceably as far as it depends on you. This means if you find yourself yelling, you probably aren't doing the best job of living peaceably. Maybe you avoid this situation in general and you have decided to never associate with "sinners." This too would be wrong. You can't bring peace if you never approach the place of conflict. We must be willing to engage with people who need the truth of Jesus. These people are spiritually sick, and they need the Great Physician to bring complete and lasting peace to their lives.

It is not our job to bring salvation, but it is our job to bring peace to these people. Hebrews 12:14 tells us why. This verse gives us a convicting word about bringing peace to unbelievers. *"Strive for peace with everyone, and for the holiness without which no one will see the Lord."*[119] Listen to these words and take them to heart. This verse says that without peace and holiness, no one will see the Lord. This is why it is so important for us to live lives that are holy and pure. I am not saying that we need to be perfect for people to see God in us, but I am saying that if we are not set apart in our words and actions, we will make it hard for unbelievers to see Jesus in and through us. In the same way, if we do not live in peace with others, no one will see the Lord through us. They might see Jesus through other believers, but not through us, if we are not living a life of peace and holiness.

This is the good news. Romans 5:6-8 says, *"For while we were still weak, at the right time Christ died for the ungodly. For one will scarcely die for a righteous person—though perhaps for a good person one would dare even to die—but God shows his love for us in that while we were still sinners, Christ died for us."*[120] So, if we have taken hold of this truth, how much more should we be willing to bring peace to those who have not yet experienced the peace of God? Jesus came into the world to save sinners like you and me, and also for the person who you refuse to try to make peace with. If we find ourselves at any point thinking the other person is not worthy of the peace of God, or that they should be left alone to live a life they choose, we are obviously not caring about that person. Think about how you would feel if someone decided that about you when you were an unbeliever. The fact is that we are all unworthy of the peace of God. We all deserve to die in our sin, but God loves us so much that he made a way through Jesus for us to have peace forever; peace with God, and peace within ourselves. Now it is our part to bring and offer that peace to the world around us because Christ died for the ungodly.

Jesus clearly calls us to bring this peace to the world, and live peaceably with others; because Jesus was different. Jesus is quaintly named the "Prince of Peace" by the prophet Isaiah. This seems fitting from the commands that he gives, as well as the eternal peace that he brings through salvation. But there is a time when Jesus is speaking to his disciples when sets the record straight. In Matthew 10:34, Jesus says to his disciples, *"Do not think that I have come to bring peace to the earth. I have not come to bring peace, but a sword."*[121] We need to add some context here. Jesus is commissioning his disciples two by two and commands them in verse 8, *"Heal the sick, raise the dead, cleanse lepers, cast out demons. You received without paying; give without pay."*[122] Jesus is essentially telling them to go and bring peace to people who are living in chaos. He also reminds them that they received this peace free of charge, therefore they are to offer this peace free of charge to others. Jesus then makes it known that he is fully aware that some will not welcome this peace. He tells them how much they will be persecuted (which is a lot), but reassures them that they have nothing to fear because they have a Father who loves and values them more than they could ever imagine.

The disciples are probably having mixed emotions right about now because they have been told the good and bad news about their mission. At this point, Jesus tells them that he didn't come to bring peace. Wait a minute… the Prince of Peace, who preaches peace, didn't even come to bring peace? Not only that, but he says that he actually came to bring a sword. This seems opposite to what he has taught, but it's not.

Jesus taught his disciples throughout his whole ministry that following him would separate them from others. Even for us now, he says that when we follow him, we'll be hated by all, thus separating us from others. Jesus is telling us that he knows that we are going to face trials of division because Jesus himself brings divisiveness. When you make the decision to follow Jesus, there will be family members or even close friends who know you better than anyone else that will ridicule you. Jesus is saying that he knows these things are true. There will always be the sword of truth, and that is the truth of God will divide people. While the truth of Jesus sets us free, the truth of sin will also be someone's ruin. We must be ready for the severance when it happens, but we are not the ones that do the cutting; this is the role of God.

Our role is to live peaceably among all as far as it is up to us. Jesus was so different in the way that he treated people. He might have come to bring a sword, but we have all seen Jesus as one who brings peace. When Peter decided to use a literal sword, Jesus brought peace by healing the man. Jesus brought peace intentionally, but the sword was at work in the background. He offered peace, shalom, wholeness, welcome, and wellbeing to the hurting world around him. While Jesus was the Prince of Peace, he was wielding a sword; but Jesus didn't lead with the sword, and neither should we.

1. Is your first instinct to bring peace or a sword to a conversation with an unbeliever?
2. Are you willing and able to bring peace without compromising the truth of scripture?

CHAPTER 9

Consistent and Persistent

*"The sluggard craves and gets nothing,
but the desires of the diligent are
fully satisfied" Proverbs 13:4* [123]

There is a big difference between being a lazy person and being lazy for a certain amount of time or instance. I think that we all are lazy at times; in fact, I know that we are, but that doesn't mean we are all lazy people at our core. You can probably think of a lazy person off the top of your head. This person has a lifestyle and general being of laziness. In the Bible, this person is described as a sluggard. A sluggard is not someone who just has a moment of laziness, but is a habitually lazy person.

Habits are fairly difficult to form, whether breaking a bad habit or forming a good one. Studies show that it takes

Consistent and Persistent

between 18-254 days to form a new habit.[124] This means it could take up to eight months of consistently doing (or not doing) something in order for a habit to form. Maybe you think this would be an easy thing to do, but I would bet that it's harder than you think. The rule of thumb used to be that it only took 21 days to form a habit. In 2023, a study group researched how many people stuck to their New Year's resolutions after 21 days. They found that only 9% of people were successful at the 21 day mark.[125] This doesn't mean that 91% of people are lazy, but it does show that habits are harder to form than we think.

To form a habit, it takes consistency. If you aren't consistent in your actions then you will never form a habit or routine. Proverbs 13 shows the truth of the human condition when it comes to laziness and consistency. It clearly teaches that we all crave and desire things in life. Hopefully we are desiring the right things, namely Jesus. But this Proverb shows there are two kinds of people—the sluggard and the diligent. One gets nothing, and the other is fully satisfied. Obviously we all want to be fully satisfied, but we don't all want to put in the work to get there.

The Shawshank Redemption is regarded as one of the best movies ever made. It is a story of a man named Andy Dufresne, who was wrongly convicted of the murder of his wife and her adulterous lover.[126] The story follows Andy's time in prison among some pretty brutal prisoners. He has no choice but to make the most of his situation.

Andy was a very persistent and consistent man. At one point in the story, he luckily acquires the job of working in the prison library renting books to the prisoners. Andy wants to get some more books for his fellow prisoners to read, so in order to make this happen, he writes a letter every week to the state asking to receive funds for their library. He made it a habit to write this letter every week––he was persistent. After not hearing from the state for 312 letters, the state finally sent a letter back to Andy that said, *"Dear Mr. Dufresne, in response to your repeated inquiries, the state has allocated the enclosed funds for your library project. This is $200! In addition, the library district has generously responded with a charitable donation of used books and sundries. We trust this will fill your needs. We now consider the matter closed. Please stop sending us letters. Yours truly, J.H. McAlahney, state controller."*[127]

With a big smile on his face, Andy said, *"it only took six years."*[128] This is the kind of attitude that Andy has when he sees that his consistency and persistence paid off. He was so happy that it only took six years, which meant he was willing and prepared to keep writing letters until he got what he wanted. Imagine if Andy would have stopped after 300 letters because he lost hope. This would have been devastating, but he would have never known that only 12 more letters would have done the trick.

If you think that this is persistent and consistent, wait until you hear his *greatest* feat. Now, this is a spoiler for the whole movie, but I have to mention it. When Andy entered the prison, he quickly found someone that could smuggle in a rock hammer for him. A rock hammer is like a tiny pickaxe that is used to carve rocks. He told his friend that he wanted to carve some chess pieces out of rock as a hobby, and that he needed this tool to do so. Andy struck a deal and ended up getting his rock hammer. While he did use the rock hammer to carve chess pieces, his main use for the rock hammer was to dig a hole in the wall of his prison cell in order to escape. Do you want to know how long it took him to dig a hole in the wall large enough for him to fit through? 19 years. Talk about consistency and persistence! Andy had to slowly and quietly dig little bits of concrete out of the prison wall at night time when guards were not present. Every day, when the prisoners were allowed to go out into the prison yard, he would take the small rocks outside to dispose of them in order to hide the evidence that he was digging a hole. He had this routine for 19 years of his life, and after 19 years, he gained his freedom. Andy Dufresne was consistent in the small things that ultimately made him a free man.

For us, it's hard to do something for 21 days, much less 19 years. Imagine being able to say that you have done something every day for the last 19 years. How good would you be at that thing? How far along would you be? I have always wanted to be bilingual, but I have yet to put in the time and energy to consistently practice learning a new language. As the Proverb says, I crave, but I get nothing.

There is something known as the 100 hour rule. This comes from a study that shows anyone who spends 100 hours practicing a certain skill will become competent in that skill.[129] This does not mean that they will be an expert, but it means that they will be able to enjoy and contribute with this new skill. According to the 100 hour rule, this means that if you practice a skill for 18 minutes per day for a year, then you will succeed in learning competence in this new skill. Only 18 minutes per day, how hard could that be? We can all find 18 minutes in our day to dedicate to learning something new. This study shows that if you have the consistency to do this, you will be in the top 5% of people in the world at that particular skill.[130] Obviously this has some gray areas, and to someone who has been honing their skills for 10 plus years, you will look like an absolute rookie. But to the person who has not taken any time to even attempt this skill, you will seem like an expert. I wonder, if this rule were to be applied to our spiritual life, what would the outcome be?

I think of all of the people I know who say that they are a Christian, and it's a lot of people. Then I think about how many of them seem like they have a deep and unwavering faith, with evidence of them putting ample time and effort into their walk with Christ. The answer is few––very few. Do you know the song Chopsticks on the piano? The one that everyone who can't actually play piano can still play. Just because you can play Chopsticks on the piano doesn't mean that you are a pianist. A real pianist would roll their eyes if you said that you were a pianist and then played the only song you know––*Chopsticks*.

This is the skill difference that I am trying to convey. James 2:19 says, *"You believe that God is one; you do well. Even the demons believe—and shudder!"*[131] James is saying there is more to following Jesus than a faith that is not actively pursuing Jesus. James knows that we are justified by grace through faith; he knows that there is nothing that we can do to save ourselves; he knows that there is nothing that we can bring to the table but our sin; and still he says in the very next verse, *"Faith apart from works is useless."*[132] James is telling us that learning to play Chopsticks isn't the end-game for our journey; it's only the beginning. When you put your faith in Jesus as the Son of the living God who died for the forgiveness of your sins, this is just the beginning of your faith journey. You don't make this decision of faith and then go back to your old life, only remembering this as a moment in your life when you simply said a prayer. Nope––at that moment, you became a new creation. The old is gone forever, but the new life with Christ has come.

I want to talk about how we can grow in following Jesus using persistence and consistency. I have broken it down into four different ways to grow. These four ways are to bring yourself to Jesus, bring people to Jesus, bring Jesus to people, and to bring people with you to Jesus. I believe that if we are persistent and consistent in doing these four things, then we will have a deeper level of intimacy with Jesus.

Let's start with talking about bringing *yourself* to Jesus. A former teacher and mentor of mine used to tell me to have a well-worn path to the tree of life. He would share about how at times you might be blinded by the world, crippled by sin, and weary from pouring out so much, and at that moment we need to know how to get back to the tree of life; even when we are blind, crippled, and weary. He said the only way that we could make it is if we had a well-worn path to the tree of life––a path that we had walked so many times before we could get there by heart. We wouldn't need our eyes to see the path because we were so used to making the trek, and even when crippled or tired, we knew that when we arrived at the tree of life that it would bring rest and healing to our lives. Jesus is that tree of life. He is the one who we need to consistently commune with, as he is the giver of life.

I love how the verse from John 15 explains it when Jesus says, *"Abide in Me, and I in you. As the branch cannot bear fruit of itself, unless it abides in the vine, neither can you, unless you abide in Me."*[133] We cannot bear fruit on our own. Because of this, it's imperative that we stay connected to the source of life. A branch apart from the vine will die. In the same way, if we are not consistently abiding in Jesus, we will spiritually die. This is why the first and most important point that we must consider is that we need to persistently and consistently bring ourselves to Jesus; because without this, we can do nothing.

Secondly, we need to persistently and consistently bring *people* to Jesus. If you are consistent in bringing yourself to Jesus, this one should come somewhat naturally. What I mean when I say bring people to Jesus is to pray for people. Prayer, in my opinion, is one of the most underutilized tools in our faith. We have direct access to the God of the universe, yet we rarely set aside time to pray. John Calvin says, *"To make intercession for men is the most powerful and practical way in which we can express our love for them."*[134]

Praying for others is a huge ministry in itself. We are typically self-centered people. When we go to the Lord in prayer, we predominantly pray for ourselves. I know that I have struggled with this myself. I don't have much of a problem bringing myself to God, but I find myself praying a lot about myself and not so much for others. I believe that praying for others is one of the best ways to love them, because as we pray for them, Jesus is interceding on their behalf. Loving people is the second greatest commandment behind loving God himself, so I believe that we should take this part of our prayer life very seriously. Matthew 5:44 even tells us to do this for those who probably don't even love us in return, saying, *"But I tell you, love your enemies and pray for those who persecute you."*[135] Just think about the impact that this would have on you. Praying consistently and persistently for others would make your heart grow for them. Jesus already loves them far more than we could ever imagine, and he loves that we are growing in our love for them as well.

Maybe they are not your enemies, but your close friends or fellow brother or sister in Christ. We should constantly be praying for them as well. Paul says many times in his letters that he always remembers them in his prayers. This is what love looks like in a spiritual prayer life; to be consistent in prayers for others. In fact, James 5:16 says, *"Therefore confess your sins to each other and pray for each other so that you may be healed. The prayer of a righteous person is powerful and effective."*[136] Our prayers for others can actually bring healing to them through intercessory prayer.

This verse also gives us some encouragement that we probably need. It says, *"The prayer of a righteous person is powerful and effective."* Sometimes, it's easy to feel like our prayers aren't heard or they are useless; but this is saying that they are powerful and effective. However, there is a contingency. It states that "the prayer of a righteous person" is powerful and effective. This righteous person is in reference to a believer and follower of Jesus. We all know that the Bible says there is no one who is righteous (Romans 3:10), but the Bible also says that we are made righteous through Christ Jesus (2 Corinthians 5:21).[137] So, James is saying that the prayers of a believer and follower of Jesus are powerful and effective, not because of the person, but because of the God whom they are praying to.

Praying for our brothers and sisters and even our enemies will keep them in the forefront of our minds. It reminds us that they are all hopeless and helpless without Jesus. Bringing them to Jesus in prayer will help move our hearts to action to reach these people for Jesus, especially when praying for our enemies. It will make us realize that we were once lost, but now we are found, and they can be too. Bringing them to Jesus in prayer will help us be selfless in our prayers, giving us an opportunity to see God move in their lives in amazing ways through faithful prayer.

Next we need to bring Jesus to *people*. Now, we have already talked about evangelism and using our words to share the gospel, so I won't go too deep into that again.

But how many times do we pray for someone and never put any action behind our prayers? Maybe you are praying for your regular barista at Starbucks every night consistently: *"Lord, please send someone to share with them about you Jesus."* Wake up! You are the person that God is sending to share with them about Jesus! Sometimes we just need to muster up the courage to have a conversation. Imagine this scenario. You have been praying for someone for months, and when you finally decide to actually talk to them about Jesus, they are fully receptive. They tell you that they have been feeling like something was missing in their life but they weren't sure what it was, so they decided to start praying to a God that they don't even know if they believe in, asking him to send someone to talk to them about God if he is real. Jesus would literally be answering both of your prayers by one simple act of obedience in reaching out to that friend and opening up a conversation about Jesus!

If we are persistent and consistent in bringing Jesus to people, a few things will happen that will change your walk with Jesus. First, you will grow in your boldness. Even if you get turned down or persecuted, sharing your faith with others always yields a blessing. The blessing comes from knowing that you have been faithful and obedient to the call of Jesus. Bringing people to Jesus also makes you more aware of the need in the world for Jesus. I live in Fort Myers, Florida. In 2019, the Barna research group determined that our city was the 14th post-Christian city in America.[138] This study looked at 16 criteria, which identified a lack of Christian identity, belief, and practice. So, when I say that I understand the potential of people around you not caring about Christian beliefs, I mean it. It's not easy to enter into these conversations knowing that it might be met with hostility, but that is not the way to think. We must think about the potential that this person may accept the call of God to follow Jesus, both now and into eternity.

Now, this next part might take some extra persistence. We need to bring people *with us* to Jesus. Most times when you share the gospel with someone for the first time, they don't immediately understand and dive right into deeper conversion. It often takes a few times—no, *many* times—sharing the gospel and carefully explaining it until they understand and commit to following Jesus. In the parable of the sower found in Matthew chapter 19, Jesus explains to them why some of the people do not receive or believe the good news of Jesus. In verse 19 Jesus says, *"When anyone hears the word of the kingdom and does not understand it, the evil one comes and snatches away what has been sown in his heart."*[139] So, these people heard the gospel yet they did not understand it, and because they did not have someone to explain the gospel persistently and consistently, the enemy took away the seed of the gospel sown to them. This is why it is so important to be persistent and consistent, because it is so rare that it takes root from the beginning. But even if they do receive the word with joy, the parable says that over time when they see that life with Jesus is not exactly the easiest life, they bail.

This is where being consistent and persistent comes in through discipleship. Discipleship looks like bringing people with you to Jesus. I look at discipleship as a way to show and teach someone else how to follow Jesus. We are there to guide them towards what the Bible says we are called to. This is when they will learn about all of the things that they were unaware of when they responded to the gospel. We must be persistent in reaching out to these people, asking when and where they need guidance. Answer any questions they have, ask what they have been learning from Jesus, hear about what they have been reading in scripture lately, or listen to how you can pray for them. Jesus knew that if we aren't consistent and persistent in this, the enemy will do his best to pull people away from him.

Jesus was different because he understood these things, he taught them, and he practiced them regularly. Jesus shows us how we can grow in our relationship with God through being consistent and persistent in our relationship with Jesus and others' relationships with Jesus through discipleship. I want to challenge you in these four practices. I am confident that if you do these things, you will grow in your faith and Jesus will show you greater things. But please, focus most on the first practice of bringing yourself to Jesus. Without this one, the others will be fruitless, and you will likely get frustrated. Be consistent and persistent in bringing yourself to Jesus, seek first his Kingdom, and the rest will be added to you.

1. Where do you see inconsistencies in your walk with Jesus?
2. What is a goal that you would like to set for yourself in order to grow spiritually?
3. In six months' time, would you rather have six months' worth of excuses or six months' worth of experience?

CHAPTER 10

Hell Is Real

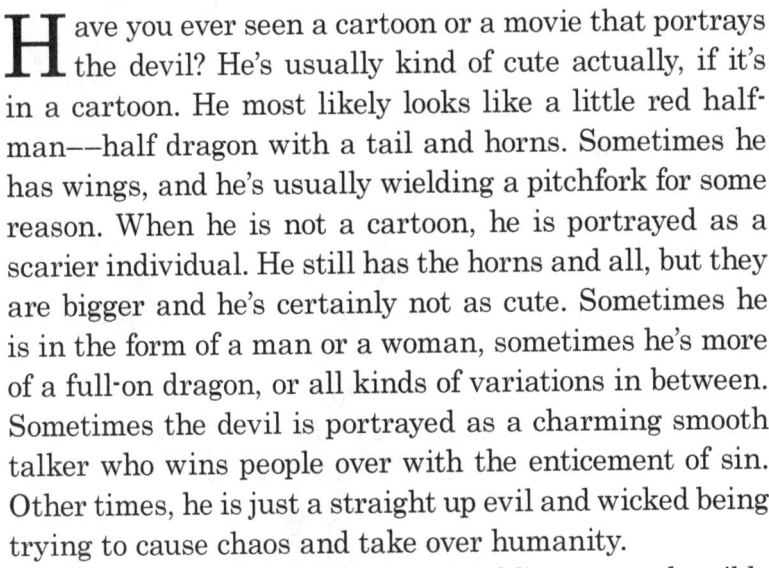

Have you ever seen a cartoon or a movie that portrays the devil? He's usually kind of cute actually, if it's in a cartoon. He most likely looks like a little red half-man––half dragon with a tail and horns. Sometimes he has wings, and he's usually wielding a pitchfork for some reason. When he is not a cartoon, he is portrayed as a scarier individual. He still has the horns and all, but they are bigger and he's certainly not as cute. Sometimes he is in the form of a man or a woman, sometimes he's more of a full-on dragon, or all kinds of variations in between. Sometimes the devil is portrayed as a charming smooth talker who wins people over with the enticement of sin. Other times, he is just a straight up evil and wicked being trying to cause chaos and take over humanity.

While some of these portrayals of Satan are plausible

and based off of scripture, there is one portrayal that I haven't mentioned that is a norm across the board, but it is totally false, which is that the devil rules over his humble abode called hell. Almost every movie, TV show, or cartoon that I have seen where the devil is a character has him almost always in hell during his scenes. But the hell that he is in seems to be his comfy little world that he is happily in charge of. This is where they get it wrong, but we will get to more of that later.

You see, less and less people even believe that hell or the devil exists. A recent Gallup poll from 2023 found that only 59% of people believe in hell, and only 58% believe that the devil is a real spiritual entity.[140] This shows that people are ignorant at best, and at worst they are ignoring the reality of Satan and hell. If you have ever seen the movie *The Usual Suspects*, you can probably recall the famous quote from the character Keyser Söze: "The greatest trick the devil ever pulled was convincing the world he did not exist." [141] No one really wants to believe that there's a real devil who is actively trying to cause chaos, much less trying to steal, kill, and destroy.

Here's the truth: the devil is real, and he hates God because he wants to be God. But he can never and will never be anything even close to God. The devil is actually fighting a losing battle with God, and he knows it. You know who else he hates? *You.* He hates you and he hates the rest of humanity. The devil wants to kill you spiritually and physically.

1 Peter 5:8 says, *"Be sober-minded; be watchful. Your adversary the devil prowls around like a roaring lion, seeking someone to devour."*[142] You might wonder, *why?* Why does the devil hate me? He hates you because you were made in the image of God. The devil knows that he can't touch God, so he attacks God's image-bearers—you

and I. The devil has zero chance at having eternal life with Jesus, but he knows that the rest of humanity does have that opportunity. No matter what you believe about predestination and election, I think we can at least agree that the devil also has no idea who is or isn't predestined or elected. Because of this, we can assume that he is going to attack every single person on the planet, trying his best to take away their opportunity of salvation.

The devil must be extremely frustrated in his pursuits, because he is operating under God's sovereign rule. This means that God has the ultimate authority and control, even over what the devil can and can't do. This is a hard one to explain, and I am not going to dive into a deep theological discussion; but I will try to help you understand this idea briefly. It's as if the devil is on a leash. He can only go as far as the Lord will let him, and he can only do what God allows.

This is one of the theological debates that opens up deeper discussions, like why God allows bad things to happen, or why he doesn't just kill the devil immediately, once and for all. While these are great things to consider, they may be better suited for another book more focused on that topic. While thinking about this can be unsettling, it should be a thought that actually brings us great comfort, because we know that God is in control.

Now, let's talk a bit about hell. Remember how all of the visual media portrays hell as the devil's little lair that he rules over? It's portrayed as if the devil has built this swanky underworld where he leads his fellow rebels to live in sin happily ever after. This is complete nonsense. The devil did not create hell; God created it. He created it for the devil, but the devil isn't looking forward to it. Matthew 25:41 says *"Depart from me, you cursed, into the eternal fire prepared for the devil and his angels."*[143] Contrary to popular belief, the devil does not want to be in hell engulfed by eternal fire. Hell was made as a punishment for the devil and his followers. The devil is simply on death row awaiting his eternal sentence in hell.

Jesus spoke a lot about hell. In fact, he talked about hell more than anyone else in the Bible. He shared about hell to both his followers and people who chose not to follow him. He did not decide to only talk about hell around believers or non-believers, but he thought that it was very important for both to hear and receive this message. His message was straight forward: hell is a real place full of God's wrath and punishment.

There are many ways that hell is described in the Bible. Some passages say that hell is where there is weeping and gnashing of teeth. It is a place full of sadness and anxiety. Have you ever been so anxious that you were in tears? Or so stressed that you found yourself grinding your teeth? That would be a normal occurrence in hell.

The Bible also says that hell is like utter darkness. Most people have some form of fear. Being afraid of the dark is a pretty normal fear, even among adults. The fear is not really about the dark, but rather the unknown that might be lurking in the dark. The Bible doesn't just say hell is dark, though; it says that hell is a place of utter darkness, meaning no light at all. This must provoke even more anxiety, meaning more weeping and gnashing of teeth.

We all probably picture hell as a place full of flames like we see portrayed in movies, and this would be somewhat correct. One of the most used descriptors of hell taken from the Bible is some form of fire. For instance *fiery furnace, lake of fire, unquenchable fire,* or *eternal fire.* Have you ever been burned by fire or something that was hot? I know I have. It is one of the most painful and uncomfortable feelings that you could ever experience. Now imagine being in a fiery furnace or being thrown into a lake of fire that cannot be quenched... *forever.* This would be complete agony for even one second, much less for eternity. But this is what the punishment of hell is like. It's a scary and painful reality that lasts forever.

Jesus even says in Matthew 10:28, *"And do not fear those who kill the body but cannot kill the soul. Rather fear him who can destroy both soul and body in hell."*[144] We should have a healthy fear of God, being that he is the Judge that sentences his wrath on unbelievers. Psalm 96:13 says, *"Before the Lord, for he comes, for he comes to judge the earth. He will judge the world in righteousness, and the peoples in his faithfulness."*[145] Jesus will judge the world with his righteousness, meaning he will make the right judgment in his verdict. This can also be comforting for us, because it says that he will judge us in his faithfulness to keep his promise to those who have put their trust in Jesus as Savior and follow him as Lord. John Piper puts it quite nicely: *"The reason we do not live in the discomfort of constant fear is because we believe."* [146] We can take comfort in knowing that our Judge is our loving God, and he is the one whom we have put our faith in for salvation through Jesus.

We have this incredible truth that Jesus came to die for the sins of the world, rose again on the third day, and then ascended into heaven. Now that we have this truth, we must prepare ourselves for this second truth that was given by angels to the disciples immediately after Jesus ascended into heaven. Recorded in the book of Acts, the angel said, *"Men of Galilee, why do you stand looking into heaven? This Jesus, who was taken up from you into heaven, will come in the same way as you saw him go into heaven."*[147] There will be a second coming from Jesus, but this time it will be to take believers home to heaven. We find this in many places of scripture, one of those being John 14:1-3: *"Let not your hearts be troubled. Believe in God; believe also in me. In my Father's house are many rooms. If it were not so, would I have told you that I go to prepare a place for you? And if I go and prepare a place for you, I will come again and will take you to myself, that where I am you may be also."*[148] Jesus has ascended into heaven to prepare a place for you and me as believers and followers of Jesus. The even better news is that he says he's coming back to get us and he will take us home. What a beautiful thought to think that Jesus is currently—right now, with love—preparing heaven for our arrival!

Let me encourage you with one more verse that gives a play-by-play of what will happen. 1 Thessalonians 4:16-17 says, *"For the Lord himself will descend from heaven with a cry of command, with the voice of an archangel, and with the sound of the trumpet of God. And the dead in Christ will rise first. Then we who are alive, who are left, will be caught up together with them in the clouds to meet the Lord in the air, and so we will always be with the Lord."*[149] I especially love the last line of this verse: *"so we will always be with the Lord."* To this I say, amen!

While Jesus will take all of those who are in Christ to be with him forever, it begs the question, *what happens to those who are not in Christ?* Well, the Bible tells us about this, too. At that time, there will be a pouring out of God's wrath in judgment against those who are not believers in Christ Jesus. This Judgment will be a separation between the righteous and the unrighteous, the believer and the non-believer. Jesus will be righteous and just in his judgment upon each person. Matthew 25:41 says, *"Then he will say to those on his left [unbelievers], 'Depart from me, you cursed, into the eternal fire prepared for the devil and his angels."*[150] We cannot ignore what this means. This is a truth that we must understand and take to heart: those who are not in Christ are going to hell.

Matthew 24:44 gives us this warning, *"Therefore you also must be ready, for the Son of Man is coming at an hour you do not expect."*[151] Similarly, 1 Thessalonians tells us that the second coming will be "like a thief in the night."[152] The Bible is clear. There will be a time that Jesus will return and it will be unexpected. This is a warning for us to prepare ourselves and help prepare others for Jesus' return.

We need to diligently prepare ourselves for the second coming of Christ. 1 John 2:28 says, *"And now, little children, abide in him, so that when he appears we may have confidence and not shrink from him in shame at his coming."*[153] We should live lives that are worthy of the gospel, as it is instructed in the book of Philippians.[154] Not that we could ever be worthy in and of ourselves, but let us strive for purity, holiness, and Christ-likeness. How great will the day of the second coming of Christ be for those who are in Christ Jesus! Let us be prepared to stand before our God and Savior in the best way possible.

This is where Jesus was different: he warned those who were not in Christ about hell. We must recognize that Jesus gave those warnings out of his great love for people's souls. Jesus came to earth out of great love for his people. We all know John 3:16: *"For God so loved the world, that he gave his only son, that whoever believes in him should not perish but have eternal life."*[155] It was love that was the driving force of Jesus coming to earth in the first place. While this is great love, Jesus cannot deny himself; he has made a decree. Later in John chapter 3, Jesus says, *"Whoever believes in the Son has eternal life; whoever does not obey the Son shall not see life, but the wrath of God remains on him."* [156]

The wrath of God remains on every single person who is outside of Christ. This is something that we who are in Christ must take seriously. We do not know when Jesus will return for his second coming, therefore we have no time to waste. We need to tell more people the gospel of Jesus and we need to tell them ASAP. I am not telling you to preach fire and brimstone style messages to your coworkers. I am not saying to go around telling people to *turn or burn*. What I am saying is that if we are being silent about something this important, then we might as well say that we don't believe in hell either.

Let's just face the facts. Jesus spoke more about hell than anyone else because he knew what hell was. Jesus knows how terrible hell is because he created it, and he loves us so much that he came to earth to die for our sins so that we could be pardoned from our sentence of death and hell. But this is only for those who will respond in faith. It is for those who confess and believe that Jesus is who he says he is. It is for those who believe that Jesus is the only way and the only truth and the only life that we have. Outside of Jesus, we are doomed.

Leonard Ravenhill said, *"Christ came the first time to kill sin in man, but he will come a second time to kill man in sin."*[157] Jesus will come again, and it will either be the greatest day ever or the worst possible scenario based upon where someone's faith lies. When sharing the gospel, we must share both sides—and there are only two sides. Life or death. Righteous or unrighteous. Jesus or the devil. Heaven or hell.

The difference that Jesus had when it came to sharing about hell was love. I know, you might be thinking that you love people too, but it's not the same. This isn't just some kind of love that is superficial. No, this love goes much deeper than that. This is also not a fairytale love, a marital love, or a motherly love for her son or daughter; it's different and it's unexplainable. One of my favorite hymns ever is *The Love of God* by Frederick M. Lehman. It beautifully describes the love which God has for us. The first verse of the hymn describes the love by saying, *"The love of God is greater far than tongue or pen can ever tell; it goes beyond the highest star, and reaches to the lowest hell; the guilty pair, bowed down with care, God gave His Son to win; His erring child He reconciled, and pardoned from his sin."*[158]

God's love is so strong that it was moved to action; it could not stand idly by. This love demanded a response, and that response was the most humble and sacrificial thing that anyone could think to do. God would go to the furthest extremes in order for his love to reach us, and there was nothing that could stop it. I love the first line that expresses the difference of God's love and ours. We could never do it justice by writing or talking about it. His love is far greater than any of our best attempts to explain it. The third verse really drives this point home, saying, *"Could we with ink the ocean fill, and were the skies of parchment made, were every stalk on earth a quill, and every man a scribe by trade; to write the love of God above would drain the ocean dry; nor could the scroll contain the whole, though stretched from sky to sky."*[159]

What an immaculate visual that is given here by Lehman. If the ocean were filled with ink and the skies were made of paper; if every stick were a pen and every person an author; if we tried to write about God's love, we would run out of ink and paper before we could ever bring justice to the explanation of God's love!

This love that Jesus had was different from the love that we currently have for the lost. The love of Jesus knew that there was a hell awaiting the devil and sinners alike.

Jesus wanted to provide a way out for sinners who would believe and follow him. So, Jesus came to earth knowing that he was going to be rejected by many; yet he continued in love for all of humanity. During his time on earth, he gave warning because he truly loved them.

Jesus gives us the call to live differently in Luke 6:35-36 by saying, *"But love your enemies, and do good, and lend, expecting nothing in return, and your reward will be great, and you will be sons of the Most High, for he is kind to the ungrateful and the evil. Be merciful, even as your Father is merciful."*[160] Jesus was loving and kind to the ungrateful and the evil, and he calls us to do the same. Not only was Jesus different by warning people about hell, but he was different in *how* to warn people about hell—with love and compassion. If we are not warning people about hell, it is because it is so far out of our minds or because we are lacking love for people. We need to keep the truth in our minds, that there is a real hell and people are going there for eternal punishment. You will be different if you share the gospel. You will be lovingly different if you share the truth about hell. You will be lovingly different, like Jesus.

1. Think about the unbelievers in the world, but specifically the ones that you know, and pray for their salvation.
2. How does it make you feel when you think about all the unbelieving people who are going to spend eternity in hell?
3. Having read this chapter, what are you going to do about it?

CHAPTER 11

Turn the World Upside Down

When the disciples realized that Jesus actually resurrected from the dead, they were all in. They followed Jesus around and listened to him teach for years. When the day came that Jesus was nailed to the cross, they were crushed. They had put all of their faith and devotion into following this man who claimed to be the true Messiah, and then they watched him die. How would you have felt? I would have been devastated, and quite frankly, I would have felt like I was bamboozled. The rest of the disciples were feeling this way as well, but of course, this is not where the story ends.

The apostle Peter, for instance, went on quite a rollercoaster ride of emotions during the last bit of Jesus' time on earth. Peter is known for doing some great things, but also some terrible things. He walked on water, but he also sank. He had the audacity to try to rebuke Jesus, and Jesus responded by saying *"get behind me, Satan."*[161] Let's look at some of Peter's narrative pre-crucifixion to post-resurrection. We can start with the fact that Peter cut off a Roman soldier's ear trying to defend Jesus while he was being arrested. This seems like Peter is fully on board with Jesus. Then later, we read that Peter denied Jesus three times before he was crucified. So, maybe Peter *wasn't* fully convinced that following Jesus was what he wanted to do. Shortly after the crucifixion, Peter, as well as some of the other disciples, went into hiding behind locked doors. It's like they were all afraid and wanted to reconvene as a group to decide what they were going to do next now that Jesus had been killed. Peter and the rest of them didn't know what to do, but at this moment three long days later, they got the news and everything changed. Plenty more happened after this, but most importantly, Peter died a death that glorified God (this was prophesied by Jesus in John 21). The Bible doesn't say how Peter died, but tradition tells us that he was crucified upside down. Regardless of how Peter died, we know that it was glorifying to God.

So, what changed? How did Peter go from being a shameful denier of Jesus to a martyr of Christ? It all changed after the resurrection. The tomb was empty and Jesus was alive in their midst, with the holes in his hands and sides to prove it. It was at this moment that Jesus met with his disciples in the room they had locked themselves in, as recorded in John chapter 20: *"Jesus said to them again, "Peace be with you. As the Father has sent me, even so I am sending you." And when he had said this, he breathed on them and said to them, "Receive the Holy*

Spirit."[162] Jesus had fulfilled the prophecies spoken of him. He proved to the disciples that he was exactly who he said he was. He was the Messiah, the Son of the living God, and the risen King Jesus--their Savior.

When Jesus said this, he was commissioning Peter and the rest of the disciples to go and live in a way that screams, *I have seen the risen Messiah and his name is Jesus!* This gift of the Holy Spirit would be with them everywhere they went, and Jesus was sending them to share this good news with the rest of the world. Peter and the others had been with Jesus for years, but it wasn't until they saw him rise from the dead that they began to live in full abandonment to preaching the gospel. I am not saying that Peter and the disciples were not believers before the resurrection, but their beliefs were confirmed after the resurrection.

Here we are, almost two thousand years later, and we are still making disciples of Jesus. Though unfortunately, I don't think many of us resemble Peter or the other disciples. Of course we want to look like them--we want to be bold in our faith; we want to stand out and be known as Christ followers. So how do we do it? How do we begin to look more like the disciples, or better yet, more like Jesus? We have to begin to live differently. We have to actually start doing what Jesus did and start doing what he taught us to do.

As the disciples began to do this, they taught others to do the same. I.E., they took the great commission seriously. I will share the passage just to make sure that we are all on the same page. Jesus gives his disciples this command in Matthew 28:18-20: *"And Jesus came and said to them, "All authority in heaven and on earth has been given to me. Go therefore and make disciples of all nations, baptizing them in the name of the Father and of the Son and of the Holy Spirit, teaching them to observe all that I have commanded you. And behold, I am with you always, to the end of the age."*[163] They went out and made disciples of Jesus, plain and simple.

They saw first-hand how to make disciples from being a disciple of the greatest rabbi of all time, Jesus. The disciples were recollecting all of the things that Jesus had taught them in order to do two things. First, they implemented all that Jesus taught them in their own lives. Second, they taught others to do the same. Yes, it is very simple, but it is not easy.

When the disciples did this, the world took notice. The book of Acts is full of amazing stories of the apostles and their disciples living like Jesus and teaching others to do the same. Forewarning, it's a mix of incredibly joyful and treacherously sad testimonies. But this is what life often looks like when you live differently. There is one point in the book of Acts where a disciple of Jesus, Jason, is being ridiculed in front of the city authorities for following Jesus. It says in Acts 17:6-7 that *"They dragged Jason and some of the brothers before the city authorities, shouting, "These men who have turned the world upside down have come here also, and Jason has received them, and they are all acting against the decrees of Caesar, saying that there is another king, Jesus."*[164]

I absolutely love this. *These men who have turned the world upside down.* When we begin to do what Jesus taught, we will look vastly different from the world around us. We will live so differently that people will clearly be able to distinguish that we are set apart from the rest of the world. Charles Spurgeon once said, *"They said the Apostles turned the world upside down. They meant by that, that they were disturbers of the peace. But they said a great true thing; for Christ's gospel does turn the world* upside down. *It was the wrong way upwards before, and now that the gospel is preached, and when it shall prevail, it will just set the world right by turning it upside down.*"[165] It is not that the disciples were doing the wrong thing, but that they were doing the right thing. When disciples of Jesus live like Jesus, we begin to live the way that Christ intends for humanity to live.

    I am certain that if we look at our lives compared to what scripture says, we will find that there are many things we can do––or stop doing––in order to live more like Jesus. The Sermon on the Mount found in Matthew chapters 5-7 seems to be a beautiful direction of ways that we can live differently from the world around us. It's like Jesus wanted to give us a list of ways that we can turn the world upside down with our actions. I want to encourage you to read the Sermon on the Mount and identify some areas in your life that you could make changes in order to live as Jesus commands. You will look extremely different when you implement the teachings of Jesus into your everyday life; people will take notice, and they will ridicule you for it. Take this as a good sign!

    Have you ever wondered what your life would be like if you actually did all of the things that Jesus commands you to do? How beautiful and God-glorifying my life would be if I followed every command in the Sermon on the Mount? I try to live a life that follows the commands of Christ daily, and I know that there are quite a few others who are also striving to obey Christ. I also see many people who claim to follow Jesus' commands, but I don't see much effort being applied. Even worse, there are many teachers who are teaching people to obey the commands of Christ in the Bible, yet not personally practicing what they preach. Former Notre Dame College football coach, Knute Rockne, once said, *"One man practicing sportsmanship is far better than a hundred teaching it."*[166] This theory applies even better to our walk with Jesus. One man practicing the commands of Christ is far better than a hundred teaching it.

When it comes down to it, there is a harsh reality that we must face: some people value Jesus and have decided to follow him in light of the gospel, but most have not. There are two parables in scripture that paint this picture beautifully—the parable of the hidden treasure, and the parable of the pearl of great value. These parables are a combined total of three verses, but they say a lot about how people who encounter Jesus should respond. Jesus says in Matthew 13:44-46, *"The kingdom of heaven is like treasure hidden in a field, which a man found and covered up. Then in his joy he goes and sells all that he has and buys that field. Again, the kingdom of heaven is like a merchant in search of fine pearls, who, on finding one pearl of great value, went and sold all that he had and bought it."*

This parable speaks of a man who finds the Kingdom of heaven. The man found the greatest treasure or pearl that he could ever find. This wasn't just another pearl, it was incomparable to the others; it was a treasure unlike any other. The man had a chance to obtain the pearl, but he had a difficult choice to make. He could only have the pearl if he gave up all of the things that he previously deemed as valuable in order to get it. This man could have seen the great value of the Kingdom of heaven, yet consider it not valuable enough to give up everything to get it. This is what I see happening in our world today. I see many people who have found the Kingdom of heaven (the gospel of Jesus), yet they don't believe it worthy of giving up everything else in order to receive it. This is a tragedy that I see every day here in America.

The man in the parable understood the value of the Kingdom of God. For that reason, he was willing to do anything that was required of him. He did not care what people thought about him when he decided to start selling all that he had, because he knew what he had found. I am sure that he would have been questioned and ridiculed by some of his friends and family upon making this decision. I can hear it now. *Why do you want to buy that field? What's so great about that pearl? Are you deranged or just foolish?* He is not deranged, and he certainly is not foolish. The Bible talks about the cross of Christ seeming foolish to those who don't believe. This man was not focused on the world telling him what was or wasn't valuable; he was focused on the Kingdom of God. He had his mind set on heavenly things. He made radical changes and decisions in order to gain Christ. As Mark 8:36 says, *"For what does it profit a man to gain the whole world and forfeit his soul?"*[167]

This man knew that the Kingdom of heaven was worthy of his life and his life's work. He was not going to forfeit his soul to gain the world; rather, he would do the exact opposite. He would forfeit the world and all of the things that it could ever offer in order to keep his soul eternally safe with Jesus. This is scary to think about. The possibility of living life (that is short) for our own worldly gratification while forfeiting our soul eternally.

This is something that I want us to be fully aware of. The Bible is clear about the two paths of life that people have to choose from. In Matthew 7:13-14 Jesus says, *"Enter by the narrow gate. For the gate is wide and the way is easy that leads to destruction, and those who enter by it are many. For the gate is narrow and the way is hard that leads to life, and those who find it are few."*

Narrow or Wide
Hard or Easy
Life or Destruction
Few or Many

Are you one of the few or one of the many? Now, I don't have a number that we could ascribe to these words "few" and "many," but I think that they speak for themselves. There is a group (few) that will be clearly set apart from the normal (many). Have you chosen the easy route or the hard one? Does your life look like everyone else's life, or does it look vastly different? I love what A.W. Tozer said: *"Go to church once a week and nobody pays attention. Worship God seven days a week and you become strange!"*[168] Can people look at your life and tell that you are different like Jesus? This is what I want for the body of believers; this is what God wants for his church.

If and when the church lives the set apart life that Jesus calls us to, only then we will turn the world upside down. The world around us will not be able to ignore that there are a *few* people who are living differently than the *many*. But this different way of life will be full of the fruit of the Holy Spirit that is at work within us. The world will see love, joy, peace, patience, kindness, goodness, faithfulness, gentleness, and self-control among everything that we say and do. We will grow in our faith and faithfulness, and the world around us will see it. The difference will be that we are actually doing what Jesus taught us to do. We will be glorifying God with our lives, and this will be on display for the rest of the world to see.

When you value Jesus, like the man in the parable did, you will do whatever God calls you to in life. God might call you to do things that seem foolish in the mind of an unbeliever; but to you, obedience is the only option.

The Mind of A Missionary by David Joannes paints this picture well: *"The words of James Calvert, a missionary to the cannibals of the Fiji Islands in 1838, are a living example of this scripture. As they arrived at the islands, the ship's captain tried to turn Calvert back, saying, "You will lose your life and the lives of those with you if you go among such savages." To that, Calvert replied, "We died before we came here."*[169]

Calvert experienced true life and understood the value of the gospel of Jesus, and he wanted others to hear the good news and experience the same. People thought that he was insane for wanting to bring the gospel to a group of cannibals, but Calvert didn't care; he counted the cost. Calvert had died to himself and was living for Christ.

When you live like Jesus, you will be different. You will do different things that different people would never consider. You will not be normal to the world around you. I bet you'd even be different from many of the people in your church. Peter reminds us of this call to be different and set apart by quoting the Lord God himself in 1 Peter 1:15-16: *"...but as he who called you is holy, you also be holy in all your conduct, since it is written, "You shall be holy, for I am holy."*[170] Peter is reminding us that this is not just a good idea or some helpful advice, but this is a call from the mouth of God.

There are a few key verses that I have withheld from mentioning until this time. We have explored many ways that Jesus was different in the way that he lived. We also looked at some of Jesus' teachings and how different they were compared to what we usually hear and see people teaching and doing. It is obvious to see how different Jesus was, but now the question is, *can people see how different you are?* I love this quote from an old spoken word titled *Does Anybody Know That You're a Christian*: "Can *anybody tell that you're a Christian by your actions, or does everybody think that you're a Christian because you're acting?"*[171] That line always hit me hard, because for a long time in my life, I was acting. I was portraying the life of a Jesus follower while my heart was far from him. The truth is, I cared more about pleasing people than pleasing God. I would have preferred the approval of man more than the approval of God. When I fully decided to give my life to Jesus, all of that changed. Galatians 1:10 says, *"For am I now seeking the approval of man, or of God? Or am I trying to please man? If I were still trying to please man, I would not be a servant of Christ."*[172] I am now a servant of Christ, and I no longer live to serve the flesh. I live to be different. Acts 5:29 says that *"We must obey God rather than men."* This is what I want to live by. I am not perfect, nor will I ever be; but I want to live my life in obedience to Jesus and what he teaches. When Jesus teaches us to love people—even our enemies—I will love them. When Jesus says to be humble, I will humble myself. When Jesus commands us to trust him, I will cling to his truth. When Jesus asks us to spread his gospel, I will preach the good news with boldness. I will live the different life that Jesus calls me to, because Jesus lived a different life for me. And he lived a different life for you as well. Romans 5:7-8 says, *"For one will scarcely die for a righteous person—though perhaps for a good person one would dare even to die—but God shows his love for us in that while we were still sinners, Christ died for us."*[173] Jesus was willing to do the unthinkable. He died for the unrighteous, sinful, and the wretched. He died for *you*. He loves *you*. He lives for *you*. If you want to be different, be like Jesus. Do what he did and obey his commands. Jesus was different, now go and do likewise.

Notes

Notes

Notes

Notes

Notes

Notes

Notes

Notes

ENDNOTES

1. (*ESV Study Bible* #)
2. ("TIME Magazine Cover: The Jesus Revolution - June 21, 1971")
3. (*ESV Study Bible* #)
4. (*ESV Study Bible* #)
5. ("What does it mean that Jesus is God's only begotten son?")
6. (Daye)
7. (*ESV Study Bible* #)
8. (Crossway Books #)
9. (*ESV Study Bible* #)
10. (*ESV Study Bible* #)
11. (*ESV Study Bible* #)
12. (*ESV Study Bible* #)
13. (*ESV Study Bible* #)
14. (*ESV Study Bible* #)
15. (*ESV Study Bible* #)
16. (Atwood)
17. ("Ignorance Definition & Meaning")
18. ("Ignore Definition & Meaning")
19. (Partridge) (Relearn.org)
20. (*ESV Study Bible* #)
21. (Tiegreen)
22. (*ESV Study Bible* #)
23. (*ESV Study Bible* #)

24 (*ESV Study Bible #*)
25 (*ESV Study Bible #*)
26 (*ESV Study Bible #*)
27 (*ESV Study Bible #*)
28 (*ESV Study Bible #*)
29 (*ESV Study Bible #*)
30 (*Is It Cake*)
31 (*ESV Study Bible #*)
32 (*ESV Study Bible #*)
33 (*ESV Study Bible #*)
34 (*ESV Study Bible #*)
35 ("Bliss Definition & Meaning")
36 (*ESV Study Bible #*)
37 (*ESV Study Bible #*)
38 (*ESV Study Bible #*)
39 (*ESV Study Bible #*)
40 (Spurgeon)
41 (*ESV Study Bible #*)
42 (*ESV Study Bible #*)
43 (*ESV Study Bible #*)
44 (*ESV Study Bible #*)
45 (*ESV Study Bible #*)
46 (*ESV Study Bible #*)
47 (*ESV Study Bible #*)
48 ("Ride Nature")
49 ("The House Of Ride Nature")
50 ("A Call To Action Conference")
51 (*ESV Study Bible #*)
52 (*ESV Study Bible #*)
53 (Rao and Wendling)
54 (*ESV Study Bible #*)
55 (*ESV Study Bible #*)
56 (*ESV Study Bible #*)
57 (*ESV Study Bible #*)
58 (*ESV Study Bible #*)
59 (*ESV Study Bible #*)
60 (*ESV Study Bible #*)
61 (*ESV Study Bible #*)
62 ("The One Thing Needful")

63   (*ESV Study Bible #*)
64   (Jobs)
65   ("Shackleton Story – Shackleton Equity Partners")
66   (*ESV Study Bible #*)
67   (Taylor)
68   (*ESV Study Bible #*)
69   (*ESV Study Bible #*)
70   (Ravenhill)
71   (*ESV Study Bible #*)
72   (*ESV Study Bible #*)
73   (*ESV Study Bible #*)
74   (*ESV Study Bible #*)
75   (*ESV Study Bible #*)
76   (*ESV Study Bible #*)
77   ("Conquistadors - Cortés")
78   (*ESV Study Bible #*)
79   (*ESV Study Bible #*)
80   (*ESV Study Bible #*)
81   (*ESV Study Bible #*)
82   (Carollo)
83   (Lane)
84   (Tolkien #)
85   (Jackson)
86   (*ESV Study Bible #*)
87   (Ripken and Lewis #)
88   (ten Boom et al. #)
89   ("Free Burma Rangers")
90   (Manning)
91   (Duarte)
92   (Arora)
93   ("One Month On: 5 billion engaged with the FIFA World Cup Qatar 2022™")
94   (Abrahams)
95   (*ESV Study Bible #*)
96   (*ESV Study Bible #*)
97   (Abrahams)
98   (*ESV Study Bible #*)
99   (Abrahams)
100 (Abrahams)

101 (Foxe)
102 (Abrahams)
103 (Daniels)
104 (*ESV Study Bible #*)
105 (*ESV Study Bible #*)
106 (*ESV Study Bible #*)
107 (Petrie)
108 (*ESV Study Bible #*)
109 (*ESV Study Bible #*)
110 (*ESV Study Bible #*)
111 (*ESV Study Bible #*)
112 (*ESV Study Bible #*)
113 (*ESV Study Bible #*)
114 (*ESV Study Bible #*)
115 (*ESV Study Bible #*)
116 (*ESV Study Bible #*)
117 (*ESV Study Bible #*)
118 (*ESV Study Bible #*)
119 (*ESV Study Bible #*)
120 (*ESV Study Bible #*)
121 (*ESV Study Bible #*)
122 (*ESV Study Bible #*)
123 (*ESV Study Bible #*)
124 (Solis)
125 (Solis)
126 (Darabont)
127 (Darabont)
128 (Darabont)
129 (Bogel)
130 (Bogel)
131 (*ESV Study Bible #*)
132 (*ESV Study Bible #*)
133 (*ESV Study Bible #*)
134 (Calvin)
135 (*ESV Study Bible #*)
136 (*ESV Study Bible #*)
137 (*ESV Study Bible #*)
138 (Rana)
139 (*ESV Study Bible #*)

140 (Brenan)
141 (Singer)
142 (*ESV Study Bible* #)
143 (*ESV Study Bible* #)
144 (*ESV Study Bible* #)
145 (*ESV Study Bible* #)
146 (Piper)
147 (*ESV Study Bible* #)
148 (*ESV Study Bible* #)
149 (*ESV Study Bible* #)
150 (*ESV Study Bible* #)
151 (*ESV Study Bible* #)
152 (*ESV Study Bible* #)
153 (*ESV Study Bible* #)
154 (*ESV Study Bible* #)
155 (*ESV Study Bible* #)
156 (*ESV Study Bible* #)
157 (Ravenhill)
158 (Lehman)
159 (Lehman)
160 (*ESV Study Bible* #)
161 (*ESV Study Bible* #)
162 (*ESV Study Bible* #)
163 (*ESV Study Bible* #)
164 (*ESV Study Bible* #)
165 (Spurgeon)
166 (Eng)
167 (*ESV Study Bible* #)
168 (Tozer)
169 (Joannes #)
170 (*ESV Study Bible* #)
171 (Allen)
172 (*ESV Study Bible* #)
173 (*ESV Study Bible* #)

Printed in the USA
CPSIA information can be obtained
at www.ICGtesting.com
CBHW030254301024
16598CB00013B/256